STRIKING THEIR MODERN POSE

Purdue Studies in Romance Literatures

Editorial Board

Íñigo Sánchez Llama, Series Editor
Brett Bowles
Elena Coda
Paul B. Dixon

Patricia Hart
Gwen Kirkpatrick
Allen G. Wood

Howard Mancing, Consulting Editor
Floyd Merrell, Consulting Editor
Susan Y. Clawson, Production Editor
Joyce L. Detzner, Assistant Production Editor

Associate Editors

French
Jeanette Beer
Paul Benhamou
Willard Bohn
Gerard J. Brault
Thomas Broden
Mary Ann Caws
Glyn P. Norton
Allan H. Pasco
Gerald Prince
Roseann Runte
Ursula Tidd

Italian
Fiora A. Bassanese
Peter Carravetta
Benjamin Lawton
Franco Masciandaro
Anthony Julian Tamburri

Luso-Brazilian
Fred M. Clark
Marta Peixoto
Ricardo da Silveira Lobo Sternberg

Spanish and Spanish American
Maryellen Bieder
Catherine Connor
Ivy A. Corfis
Frederick A. de Armas
Edward Friedman
Charles Ganelin
David T. Gies
Roberto González Echevarría
David K. Herzberger
Emily Hicks
Djelal Kadir
Amy Kaminsky
Lucille Kerr
Howard Mancing
Floyd Merrell
Alberto Moreiras
Randolph D. Pope
Elżbieta Skłodowska
Marcia Stephenson
Mario Valdés
Howard Young

 volume 65

STRIKING THEIR MODERN POSE

Fashion, Gender,

and Modernity in

Galdós, Pardo Bazán, and Picón

Dorota Heneghan

Purdue University Press
West Lafayette, Indiana

Copyright ©2015 by Purdue University. All rights reserved.

∞ The paper used in this book meets the minimum requirements of American National Standard for Information Sciences—Permanence of Paper for Printed Library Materials, ANSI Z39.48-1992.

Printed in the United States of America
Interior template design by Anita Noble;
template for cover by Heidi Branham.
Cover photo: *Spanish fashions, Summer 1881*. Reproduced by permission from Ella Strong Denison Library, Scripps College.

Library of Congress Cataloging-in-Publication Data

Heneghan, Dorota, 1970–
  Striking their modern pose : fashion, gender, and modernity in Galdós, Pardo Bazán, and Picón / Dorota Heneghan.
    pages cm. — (Purdue studies in Romance literatures ; volume 65)
  Includes bibliographical references and index.
  ISBN 978-1-55753-725-6 (pbk. : alk. paper) — ISBN 978-1-61249-430-2 (epdf) — ISBN 978-1-61249-431-9 (epub) 1. Modernism (Literature)—Spain. 2. Spanish fiction—20th century—History and criticism. 3. Spanish fiction—19th century—History and criticism. 4. Pérez Galdós, Benito, 1843–1920—Criticism and interpretation. 5. Pardo Bazán, Emilia, condesa de, 1852–1921—Criticism and interpretation. 6. Picón, Jacinto Octavio, 1852–1923—Criticism and interpretation. 7. Fashion in literature. 8. Gender identity in literature. 9. Civilization, Modern, in literature. I. Title.
  PQ6140.M63H46 2016
  863'.609112—dc23
                              2015027354

To my wonderful husband, Joseph and my beloved daughter, Elizabeth Suzanne "Suzie," for their patience and support of this project.

Contents

- *ix* **Acknowledgments**
- 1 **Introduction**
- 21 **Chapter One**
  Fashioning Womanhood and Making Modernity in Galdós's *La desheredada*
- 41 **Chapter Two**
  What Is a Man of Fashion? Manuel Pez and the Dandy in Galdós's *La de Bringas*
- 59 **Chapter Three**
  Fashion and Feminity in Pardo Bazán's *Insolación*
- 77 **Chapter Four**
  The Sartorial Charm of the Modern Man in Pardo Bazán's *Insolación*
- 95 **Chapter Five**
  Dressing the New Woman in Picón's *Dulce y sabrosa*
- 113 **Conclusion**
- 119 **Notes**
- 131 **Bibliography**
- 149 **Index**

Acknowledgments

I owe my deepest gratitude to my professors and mentors at Yale University, Noël Valis and Rolena Adorno, for their guidance, encouragement, and consistent support of my academic endeavors. I am particularly thankful to my advisor, Professor Noël Valis, for her generosity, kindness, and stimulation of my love for the authors to whom I dedicate my academic life. A very special thanks goes to Professor Íñigo Sánchez-Llama for his meticulous reading of and critical response to this manuscript and Professor Alan Smith for his comments and suggestions for the early version of Chapter 2.

I would also like to acknowledge the professional support of my colleagues at Louisiana State University, in particular, the chairs of the department, John Pizer and Emily Batinski, throughout the process of writing this book. Summer grants from the Louisiana State University Council on Research and the Program for Cultural Cooperation between Spain's Ministry of Culture and the United States' Universities allowed me to complete my research for this project. An award to Louisiana Artists and Scholars, which was granted to me by the Board of Regents for the academic year 2011–12, made it possible to undertake final revisions and prepare this book for publication.

Part of Chapter 2, now revised and expanded, first appeared as "What Is a Man of Fashion? Manuel Pez and the Image of the Dandy in Galdós *La de Bringas*," in *Anales Galdosianos* 44/45 (2009–10): 57–70. Chapter 3 is an expanded version of "Fashion and Femininity in Emilia Pardo Bazán's *Insolación*," *Hispanic Review* 80.1 (Winter 2012): 63–84. I am grateful to the editors of these journals and the University of Pennsylvania Press for permission to reprint here. Great appreciation is also due to the Ella Strong Denison Library at Scripps College for permission to use the fashion plate *Spanish fashions, Summer 1881* from the Fashion Plate Collection on my book cover.

Finally, I thank my parents for the boundless love and unflagging support they gave me during this project and always.

Introduction

Writing about Madrid in his 1832 collection of social sketches *Panorama matritense*, Ramón Mesonero Romanos stated proudly: "a uno que hubiera dejado nuestra capital en 1802 le sería imposible reconocerla en 1832" (100). Spaniard or foreigner, a visitor to Madrid in the early 1830s would marvel at the changes in the landscape of the city: its new public buildings, lively squares and boulevards, elegant cafés, theaters, and shops. With a mass of diverse artifacts and distractions and the opulent window displays, "aquellas serpientes tentadoras" ("Los escaparates" 195), wrote Antonio Flores twenty years later, Madrid was a site of irresistible fascination. Flores's description of the window shoppers, incited to practice extravagant consumption and self-spectacle, shows that Madrid, like many other nineteenth-century Western metropolises, was home to nascent modernity and its key components: consumerism, mass culture, and urban spectacle. Two decades later, another social commentator, Ángel Fernández de los Ríos, in his depiction of new stores and the Madrilenian society's pursuit of elegance and outward sophistication, singled out one more important feature of modern life: fashion.

> [L]a sociedad madrileña es esclava de las modistas y los sastres ... basta un mes para mudar de peinado y la hechura del vestido de la mujer, desde la dama que no se ocupa más que del tocador, hasta la obrera que por el género de su ocupación tiene que rozarse con el público; no se cambia con más rapidez una prenda en el uniforme del ejército; los hombres necesitan un valor heroico para salir a la calle con sombrero de ala ancha cuando todos la estilan estrecha, con la bota de punta cuadrada cuando todos la llevan redonda: la moda impone ahora una tela de enormes y estrambóticos cuadros, y Madrid parece poblado de jergones en movimiento ... (766–67)

Introduction

The involvement of fashion in the formation of modern Spanish society did not escape the attention of nineteenth-century Spanish writers. The sparkling appearances of female and male characters in Benito Pérez Galdós's, Emilia Pardo Bazán's, and Jacinto Octavio Picón's narratives demonstrate that authors were keenly aware of the importance that dressing stylishly played in the cultural development of the Spanish bourgeois world. The skillful manipulation of sartorial features in the portrayals of their modish protagonists indicates, moreover, that the art of dressing provided them with an effective medium to voice their stance on different aspects (consumerism, urbanization, class, gender, to name only a few examples) of the evolving modern society. The purpose of this book is to demonstrate the ways in which the above-mentioned novelists used fashion to address the shifting notions of gender. Through the close examination of stylish characters' portraits in four narratives (*La desheredada* and *La de Bringas* by Galdós, *Insolación* by Pardo Bazán, and *Dulce y sabrosa* by Picón), the objective of this study is to reveal how these novelists implicated fashion in accentuating the need to reformulate the dominant ideals of gender as a necessary step toward Spain's full integration into modernity.[1]

It bears noting that the richness of sartorial details in the aforementioned writers' works (and in particular in Galdós's novels) has attracted a great deal of scholarly interest (Díaz Marcos 185–222; Anderson 49–72).[2] Yet, even in the most recent analyses, critics tend to link the depictions of the protagonists' fashionable *toilettes* to the middle class's social ambition, female vanity, and vice (Blanco Carpintero, "La indumentaria"; Muñoz). Supportive of these interpretations are the classic studies concerning fashion and luxury, such as Thorstein Veblen's *The Theory of the Leisure Class* (1899), Werner Sombart's *Luxury and Capitalism* (1913), and J. C. Flügel's *The Psychology of Clothes* (1930), which privilege the notion of class rivalry and emulation.[3] Equally encouraging are the countless anti-fashion accounts penned by nineteenth-century clergy and social moralists (Aldaraca, *El Ángel del Hogar* 100–08; Jagoe, *Ambiguous Angels* 87–90). Finally, there are the observations by progressive nineteenth-century commentators and writers, who at times also aired their concerns about the effects of dressing *à la mode* on the confusion of classes, the democratization of luxury, and the sartorial pretentiousness of the Spanish middle class. "La clase media, compuesta de empleados o *proletarios decentes* sacada de su quicio y lanzada en medio de la aristocracia por la confusión de clases, a la merced de un frac, nivelador universal de los hombres del siglo XIX, se cree en la clase alta," complained Mariano José de Larra in "Jardines públicos" (1834) (246–47; Larra's italics). Similarly, the social commentator José Selgas in the essay "Vista exterior," published in his collection of social sketches, *Fisonomías contemporáneas* (1877), was stupefied over society's frenzy for sartorial opulence and ostentation. "En nada se advierte tanto el espíritu a la vez democrático y aristocrático de nuestro siglo como en el prosaico ropaje con que cubrimos nuestras personas. Confieso … que en algunas ocasiones no he sabido distinguir un lacayo de un duque" (14). Lastly, the fraudulent manipulation of external appearances was a recurrent topic in Galdós's narrative. In *Tormento* (1884), for example, the author offers a portrayal of Madrilenian society in which everyone (particularly women) strives to dress fashionably in order to look wealthy: "Las niñas … cuanto más pobres más soberbias … son … unas gastadoras, y no piensan más que en divertirse y en ponerse perifollos. En los teatros ves damas que parecen duquesas, y resulta que son esposas de tristes empleados que no ganan ni para zapatos" (108).[4]

There is no doubt that the middle class's rampant desire for dressing chic betrays social aspiration. After all, the period of transition to modernity was, as the above comments indicate and as scholars have commented (Sieburth 39), the era of pretense and class confusion, which created opportunity for newcomers to assert their desired social identity via dress. Yet, to assume that Spanish bourgeois men and women dressed trendy *only* to mark their position in society is to ignore the influence of fashion on other aspects of their lives. In recent years, scholars drew attention to cultural practices of the nineteenth-century bourgeoisie as fertile terrain for exploring "struggles that characterized Spain's uneven process of transitioning into modernity" (Jesus Cruz 14). Since Spain's modernization and the transformation of bourgeois culture into a hegemonic culture was a long and complex process, the everyday aspects of middle class lifestyle: their manner of dressing, shopping habits, enjoyment of leisure, offer innovative perspectives on the ways in which the nineteenth-century Spanish bourgeoisie participated in the construction of modern society and negotiated their places within it (J. Cruz 1–19). It is true

Introduction

that to discuss the middle class pursuit of elegance in relation to gender also means to analyze the richness of their modish *toilettes* from only one angle. Additionally, as Galdós's, Pardo Bazán's, and Picón's positions on the shifting gender norms were diverse and ambivalent, the examination of the sartorial portraits of their protagonists does not represent the definitive word on the subject. Instead, this study seeks to add new insights into the problematic formation of modern femininity and masculinity in Spain and the ways in which the above-mentioned authors tied the issues of gender to their views on the country's progress toward modernity.

The interrelation between fashion, gender, and modernity has become a popular subject of investigation in recent years. It was Baudelaire, of course, who, in his famous essay "The Painter of Modern Life" (1863), first addressed the relationship between fashion and modernity. Later on, Walter Benjamin (Gilloch 128–34; 240–42), following Georg Simmel (Frisby 95–101), expanded upon the connection between the ephemeral, transient beauty of the sartorial art and the enigmatic charm of the fast-paced rhythm of modern life. Since then, various scholars (Moers; Cunnington; Hollander, *Seeing through Clothes*) have drawn attention to the richness in designs and vitality of the sartorial art as a hallmark of changing ideals of femininity and masculinity. Lately, research by Elizabeth Wilson, particularly her study *Adorned in Dreams: Fashion and Modernity* (1985), has inspired an increasing number of scholars to recognize fashion as a key feature of modernity and to delve into its effects on the construction and representation of gender, both social (Evans and Thornton; Breward; Entwistle and Wilson; Buckley and Fawcett) and literary (Garelick; Feldman; Felski).

Critics of Galdós and Pardo Bazán (but unfortunately not so many of Picón) also have shed light on the rapidly developing modern consumerism in Spain and the manner in which these writers availed themselves of the metaphor of fashion to challenge established notions of gender. Kathleen E. Davis, for instance, dedicated her study to the pro-consumerist discourse on the articles by Spanish fashion critic Blanca Valmont during the 1880s and 1890s. In it, Davis examined the echoes of pro-materialist arguments in Galdós's portrait of the female protagonist in *Lo prohibido* (1888) as the main character attempts to reconcile the characteristics of a modern shopper with those of the traditional domestic angel. Likewise, Akiko Tsuchiya, in her recent work on gender deviance, identified consumerism in *La desheredada* (1881) as a potential space for female agency and resistance to established notions of femininity. Finally, Joyce Tolliver's ("'La que entrega'") and most recently Martha E. Davis's investigations (even though they are centered on Pardo Bazán's modernist short fiction) provided insight into the employment of fashionable details in doña Emilia's critique of gender inequality, particularly with respect to the prevalent attitudes toward sex and feminine sexuality.

In my approach to the portraits of the fashionable male and female characters in the novels by Galdós, Pardo Bazán, and Picón, I draw on both: research that does not necessarily relate to the Spanish narrative, and scholarship that links the construction of gender to the art of dressing and modern consumer culture in late-nineteenth-century Spanish fiction. For example, Ellen Moers's classic study on dandyism and the ensuing examination of the figure of the dandy by Rhonda Garelick are essential to my analysis of the male character in Galdós's *La de Bringas* in Chapter 2. Both works enabled me to shed light on the much-denied bourgeois male interest in fashion. They drew my attention to the way in which nineteenth-century Spaniards conformed to and, simultaneously, diverged from the conventional model of their gender through the details of their modish apparel and the repertoire of premeditated postures and gestures. Additionally, Kathleen E. Davis's research on the pro-consumerist discourse and nineteenth-century journalists' and writers' efforts to balance modern consumer values with domestic ideology provided me with a wealth of material and contextual framework for Chapter 1. My own reflections on Pardo Bazán's use of fashionable details in her male and female protagonists' portraits that allowed her to reinforce and to stretch the limits of traditional femininity and masculinity in Chapters 3 and 4 were stimulated by Tolliver's in-depth analysis of the alternation of narrative voices and perspectives in *Insolación*. Equally thought-provoking were her studies of the lexical expressions and linguistic structures in doña Emilia's short stories as modes of the author's articulations of her critical views on restrictive—especially for women—bourgeois sexual mores.

Additionally, the theoretical framework that comes from the work of Celia Amorós, Toril Moi, and Max Weber is supportive of this investigation. Amorós's thought that a truly democratic

Introduction

project requires participation of fully autonomous subjects of both genders threads through all the chapters of this book as all three novelists shared the view that the reconfiguration of traditional ideals of femininity and masculinity was a necessary condition for Spain to advance—in a tangible way—with the process of modernization. Amorós's analysis of the incompleteness of modernity in the context of the outcome of the French Revolution, which denied women the right to claim the status of individuals, rational subjects, and active citizens, is illuminating with respect to Galdós's presentation of female struggle for agency via fashion in *La desheredada*. Although Amorós centers her discussion in a cultural setting that is different from late-nineteenth-century Spain, her observations are useful in understanding Galdós's disappointment with the results of the Revolution of 1868 and his position on the effects of failure to provide women with new—real—spaces of subjectivity on the country's uneven transition to modernity. Toril Moi's essay "What Is a Woman?," based on her revision of Simon de Beauvoir's *The Second Sex* (1949), foregrounds the idea (present in all chapters of this book dedicated to the formation of modern femininity) that a woman (much like fashion itself) is never a fixed reality but rather an open-ended becoming, continuously in the process of making herself. Following de Beauvoir, Moi emphasized that the female body is not a passive object that alone defines a woman. Although Moi did not deal with dress, the concept of a woman using her corporeality as her style of being in the world and as her perspective on it, sheds light on the ways in which female protagonists in Galdós's, Pardo Bazán's, and Picón's narrative engaged their stylish bodies as a medium through which they experienced and articulated their self. Finally, Max Weber's theory of the origin of modern capitalism lends insight into the connection between Galdós's portrayal of a fashionable male in *La de Bringas* and the novelist's views on Spain's problematic integration into modernity. According to Weber, attitudinal factors, stemming from the Protestant religion and work ethic, such as frugality, methodical labor, individualism, and initiative in pursuing wealth, contributed to the dissemination of the capitalist spirit in equal measure with technological innovations and industrial progress. Weber's argument helps to understand Galdós's disapproval of his dandylike character in Chapter 2 and the author's position that failure to develop the above-mentioned cultural values and work ethic among middle-class Spanish men constituted as much the cause of the country's problematic entry into modernity as the insufficient economic growth and political stagnation.

Although the link between fashion, gender, and modernity did not escape scholars' attention, no book-length study has focused specifically on the art of dressing in Galdós's, Pardo Bazán's, and Picón's novels and its role in these authors' methods of questioning the hegemonic construction of femininity and masculinity.[5] The objective of my book is to fill this gap. By analyzing solely through the prism of fashion the issues of gender in these writers' works, the intent of this project is to broaden the existing research on these novelists' reactions to the shifting limits of womanhood and manhood in late-nineteenth-century Spain. Additionally, I seek to bring forward the manners in which these authors integrated their perspectives on gender matters into their views on the formation of modern society in Spain and the country's transition to modernity. First, the objective of this book is to emphasize the complexity of the fashionable female body and its connection to the uncertainties of gender, which are not always obvious to Galdós's, Pardo Bazán's, and Picón's audience. Close examination of modish female protagonists in the aforementioned narratives will show that they rarely conform to the normative representation of a nineteenth-century fashionable woman as inert, decorative, and idle. Thus, in this book I draw attention to the portrayals of the stylishly adorned female bodies not as passive reflections of voguish dressing styles of their time but as battlegrounds where, under Galdós's, Pardo Bazán's, and Picón's pens, limits of culturally accepted norms of femininity were called into question and renegotiated. Second, this work is intended to shed light on an area largely unexplored in previous studies—the male pursuit of fashion. Through the analysis of the richness of sartorial subtleties in Galdós's and Pardo Bazán's portraits of their male protagonists, this project will bring to light these writers' exposures of incoherencies and contradictions in the allegedly monolithic, stable concept of bourgeois masculinity. Finally, this study demonstrates that these authors manipulated the sartorial signs not only to voice their critique of conventional gender order but also to explore and envision (as is the case of Pardo Bazán and Picón) alternative models of masculinity and femininity. Threading through all chapters of this book is the idea that Spain's full integration into modernity

Introduction

required not only the redefinition of the feminine role but also the reconfiguration of the masculine one as well.

Why did fashion become one of the privileged means employed by Galdós, Pardo Bazán, and Picón for challenging and reformulating dominant representations of gender? What was so special about *la moda* in the 1880s and 1890s in Spain that made it integral to these writers' views on gender issues and their perspectives on the country's transition to modernity? Ana María Díaz Marcos noted that the meaning of the word *fashion* (or *la moda*) was generally unknown in Spain before the beginning of the eighteenth century. Even though, for instance, don Diego, the protagonist in Agustín Moreto's comedy, *El lindo don Diego* (1662), used the word *fashion* in his conversation with servants (Lope and Martín), it seems that only the main character understood its significance:

> DIEGO. ¡Que no aprendáis a poner los espejos a la moda!
> MARTÍN. Di cómo, y no te alborotes.
> LOPE. ¿Qué es la moda?
> DIEGO. ¡Mi rabia toda! ¡Que no sepan lo que es moda hombres que tienen bigotes! (Moreto 56)

The term *la moda* is absent from Covarrubias's early-seventeenth-century dictionary. It is defined, however, in the *Diccionario de Autoridades* in 1732 as "[u]so, modo ú costumbre. Tómase regularmente por el que es nuevamente introducido, y con especialidad en los trages y modos de vestir" (583). Moreover, as one can see from Benito Feijoo's manner of criticizing the influence of foreign dressing styles in Spain in his essay "Las Modas" (1728), the concept of fashion was well known among Spanish intellectuals in the early decades of the eighteenth century. "Nunca se menudearon tantos las modas como ahora, ni con mucho. ... Ya no se deja un modo de vestir porque fastidia, ni porque el nuevo parece o más conveniente o más airoso. Aunque aquél sea y parezca mejor, se deja porque así lo manda la moda" (Feijoo 67). Feijoo's negative attitude toward fashion was, of course, hardly uncommon in eighteenth-century culture. Discussed mostly in the context of the debate over the consumption of foreign luxuries, fashion, which Manuel Romero del Alamo calls "hermana legitima del luxo" (637), was rarely presented in a positive light. "[E]l Luxo, la vanidad, profusion y moda, son las fecundas raices que producen en los Estados civilizados males sin termino" (92), lamented Romero del Alamo in *Efectos perniciosos del lujo* (1789). Even Juan Sempere

Introduction

y Guarinos, "the Spanish Enlightenment's most eloquent defender of conspicuous consumption" (96), as Bridget Aldaraca described him, did not have anything favorable to say about fashion: "La falta de estudio, y de crianza, y de civilidad se quiere suplir con la variedad de las modas, superfluidades de los adornos ... Se cuida más de deslumbrar a la vista que de apasionar el corazón: y los grandes maestros de agradar en la sociedad son los sastres, peluqueros, y modistas" (373).[6] Yet, as Charles Kany's descriptions of the flamboyantly attired aristocrats in *Life and Manners in Madrid 1750–1800* indicated (170–267), and Rodríguez-Solís's portraits of the extravagantly dressed Spaniards from the period between 1800 and 1824 suggested, neither eighteenth- nor early-nineteenth-century Spanish men and women concerned themselves too much with conservative writers' and moralists' negative attitude toward fashion.[7] Even a cursory glance at the increasing popularity of the first fashion journals and changes in the commercial landscape of Madrid (as described so faithfully by Ramón Mesonero Romanos in his 1832 collection of social sketches, *Panorama matritense*) reveals, in fact, that the art of dressing reached new heights of splendor in the first half of the nineteenth century.[8] As time moved on, fashion became more and more entrenched in the process of modernization and its key components: consumerism, mass culture, and urban spectacle (Parsons 42–56). Correspondingly, it became more difficult for conservative writers and social commentators to diminish or ignore its influence on gender roles, family structure, and social hierarchies. Despite the censure of importance that society attached to one's stylish appearance, fashion assumed an essential role in the cultural formation of the nineteenth-century bourgeoisie and Spain's incorporation into modernity.

Given that the consumption of fashion was noticeably involved in the erosion of class distinctions and the disruption of traditional gender divides, it is only natural that Restoration novelists turned to the sartorial art to convey the uncertain boundaries of late-nineteenth-century femininity and masculinity. However, *la moda* of the 1880s and 1890s proved to be a particularly fitting medium for these authors to articulate the contradictory and multiple images of a contemporary man or woman for another reason. Because of the plethora of mass-produced articles of clothing, accessories, and beauty products, it was no longer possible to identify one dominant dressing style in the last decades of the nineteenth century. Similarly, given the range of ideas related to both genders

Introduction

(i.e., the New Woman, the shopper, the dandy, and the New Man during the same time), it was no longer feasible to view either gender as a single, unified concept. In other words, just as the growing complexity of late-nineteenth-century fashion had made it difficult to keep abreast of the rich assortment of fabrics, colors, and designs, it was similarly problematic to define and delineate the shifting contours of modern womanhood and manhood. Hence, it is no surprise that fashion—with its breath-taking, swiftly changing variety of styles, its connection to the rapidly developing modern urban world, and its potential to reinforce and to reshape conventional ideals of femininity and masculinity—became such an effective device for nineteenth-century writers to dramatize their views on questions of gender. In addition, judging by the presence of irony and ambiguity in Galdós's, Pardo Bazán's, and Picón's portrayals of their modish characters, it is safe to presume that these novelists capitalized on the common perception of fashion as a frivolous aspect of life. Since most social commentators and writers did not grant serious consideration to fashion, the sartorial muse provided the authors under discussion with protective cover to confront patriarchal notions of gender. Although fashion did not always shield them sufficiently (as was the case of Pardo Bazán) from critics' rage, it offered them, nonetheless, a platform that was safe enough to indicate the need of remodeling current ideals of womanhood and manhood as part of the project of modernization.

Galdós, Pardo Bazán, and Picón were, of course, not the only nineteenth-century Spanish writers who recognized the importance of fashion in shaping the formation of modern life. Although their colleagues assumed diverse and not always favorable attitudes on the subject matter, they were intrigued, nevertheless, by its complex nature. Gustavo Adolfo Bécquer, for example, contributed to the women's fashion magazines *El Álbum de Señoritas* and *Correo de la Moda* with various essays on the art of dressing. In the same year in which Baudelaire published "The Painter of Modern Life" (1863) and in which he recognized in the *femme à la mode* an aesthetic expression of modernity, Bécquer highlighted the mysterious grace of a fashionable woman in his article "La mujer a la moda." In it, the poet articulated, as his French colleague did, the frivolous, fleeting charm of modern beauty through the elegance of an anonymous, stylishly attired lady. Being fashionable, Bécquer wrote, "[es] el talento femenino ... frívolo y profundo a la vez, pronto en la percepción, más rápido aún en la síntesis, brillante y fugaz" (603). While Bécquer warned his audience that the fame of the *femme à la mode* is fragile and brief, for "un descuido ... un traje de escasa novedad, un adorno de mal gusto, una flor torpemente puesta, un peinado desfavorable ... pueden ponerla en ridículo y perderla para siempre" (604), he was clearly mesmerized by her sartorial beauty. Detailed depictions of ladies' modish *toilettes* in his essays *Revista de salones* (1864) and "Bailes y bailes" (1864) evince, moreover, that the bard was not only exceptionally conversant in matters of contemporary women's dressing styles but also delighted in discussing female fashion.[9]

> ¿Cómo no decir que la duquesa de Fernán-Núñez llevaba un lindo y elegante vestido de gasa blanca, adornado con cintas de raso del mismo color ... ¿Cómo no dar a nuestras lectoras una descripción ... de la *toilette* que ostentaba la elegantísima condesa Guaqui? Era una falda blanca rizada, cubierta con otra de tul blanco ... El cuerpo era de seda blanca, y de él caían cuatro largos picos, a manera de sobrefalda. ... Era el más delicioso conjunto de frescura y de novedad. ("Bailes y bailes" 635–36; Bécquer's italics)

In contrast to Bécquer, writers such as José María de Pereda and Juan Valera did not find women's pursuit of fashion appealing (Servén). Pereda, in his essay "La mujer del ciego, ¿para quién se afeita?" (1870) and later in his novel *Pedro Sánchez* (1883), described stylish women as adulterers, whereas Valera, in his narrative *Las ilusiones del doctor Faustino* (1875), labeled them as social upstarts. "Una mujer *a la moda* ... en ocasiones llega, a ser una mujer *de moda*," Pereda claimed in "La mujer del ciego, ¿para quién se afeita?" (176–77; Pereda's italics). "La que tiene por oficio hacer ostentación pública de sus atractivos morales, físicos y artificiales ... prescinde ... de sus deberes domésticos, de los derechos, de la autoridad, de la consideración, de todo lo que se refiere a su marido," Pereda further cautioned his readers (178–79).

Likewise, Leopoldo Alas (Clarín) did not exhibit much enthusiasm for fashion. Even at the end of the nineteenth century, when most writers and intellectuals considered the variety of sartorial styles an emblem of civilization, and the first famous fashion designers (Charles Worth, Jacques Doucet, and Emile Pingat) called

Introduction

themselves artists, Clarín refused the notion of fashion as an art form. "¡La moda! Esa deidad que no tuvo nombre siquiera en la Grecia de los buenos tiempos" (254), Clarín wrote in his 1895 *palique*, "Modas I." To the Asturian novelist, fashion was not a hallmark of progress, but rather a sign of poor taste. In another essay, "Modas II" (1895), Clarín explained "[l]a *moda*, sucedáneo del buen gusto para los que no lo tienen, reina del vulgo, lazarillo tiránico para los ciegos del arte," always dominates in a society "donde faltan creencias estéticas, gusto artístico" (262; Clarín's italics). Fashion, Clarín again insisted, is not an art form but a "superstición de lo bello" (262). Nonetheless, the critical attitude toward the art of dressing did not prevent Clarín from acknowledging its effects on the development of modern urban life. "No seamos hipócritas. ... Por los trajes de las señoras ... se hacen ensanches, se contratan ferrocarriles y servicios públicos, y se entierran o resucitan expedientes, y se abren o no se abren istmos" ("Modas I" 253). Likewise, the skillful manipulation of sartorial details in his narrative evinces that the author used fashion not only as a vehicle for drawing attention to specific traits of his characters but also as an expressive venue for sharing his perspectives on the shifting ideals of gender in the context of modern life. In *La Regenta* (1884–85), for example, most of Clarín's characters are described, as María del Carmen Alonso Morales has demonstrated, "a través de sus prendas" (26). The modish features of don Álvaro de Mesía's dashing apparel, for instance, strengthen the image of him as an experienced seducer. They make him look more distinguished than all other men in Vetusta and more desirable in Ana Ozores's eyes. "El frac, la corbata, la pechera, el chaleco, el pantalón ... de Mesía, no se parecían a las prendas análogas de los demás ... Se le figuraban ya todos los caballeros que andaban por allí, don Víctor inclusive, criados vestidos de etiqueta, todos eran camareros, el único señor Mesía" (2: 375).[10] Similarly, details in Clarín's portrayal of the stylish Emma Varcárcel in *Su único hijo* (1891), such as "her luxuriously adorned body, her carefully crafted ... (hairdo), her face, covered with ... (rice powder ...)" (Tsuchiya, *Marginal Subjects* 118), called attention to the protagonist's unnaturalness, and hence the end-of-the-century fear of the feminine. Correspondingly, the sartorial aspects of Bonifacio Reyes, transformed by his wife into a feminized dandy, brought to the surface the author's dramatization of the *fin-de-siècle* crisis of masculinity (Tsuchiya, *Marginal Subjects* 118).

Of course, Clarín's mixed feelings toward the sartorial muse were hardly uncommon among nineteenth-century Spanish writers. As Galdós's article for *La Prensa* from 1884 demonstrated, he too, like Clarín, recognized that the acquisition of finery was vital to the growth of the garment industry and the development of a modern urban economy. However, as the presence of such words—*capricho, frivolidad, elemento fatal*—in the same article indicated, the author of *La desheredada* was equally concerned with the dominance of fashion:

> [E]l baile de Fernán Núñez ha sido tal que de él se acordarán por muchos años los felices mortales que lo han visto. Lujo deslumbrador ... variedad increíble de trajes ... gracias y elegancia llevadas al extremo ... Muchos censuran estas fiestas por el dineral que se gasta en ellas ... Pero cualquiera que sea la cifra ... las artes e industrias suntuarias, que dan circulación y vida a inmensos capitales, no existirían sin estas demandas constantes del capricho y de la frivolidad, elemento fatal, imprescindible de toda sociedad. (qtd. in Shoemaker 70–71)

Yet fashion fascinated Galdós. While there is more than enough evidence of his disapproval of the rising middle class's bad taste and overspending on fashion, the author's critical attitude does not mean that he missed the opportunity that the art of dressing afforded him as a cultural site for playing out the contradictions of gender. My first two chapters outline Galdós's perspectives on gender through the prism of fashion within the culture of modern consumerism in *La desheredada* and *La de Bringas*. Identified as narratives of modernity (Sieburth 27; Labanyi 91), these novels are intriguing largely because of Galdós's innovative way of bringing to light the problematic formation of modern femininity and masculinity. Through his portrayals of the fashion-oriented characters' burning desire to advance the past and look modern and, at the same time, their lack of initiative and/or opportunity to break away from the dominant gender constructs, Galdós denounced Spain's irregular (at times more apparent than real) progress toward modernity.

Chapter 1, "Fashioning Womanhood and Making Modernity in Galdós's *La desheredada*," traces the methods in which the author deployed sartorial images in the portrait of his protagonist Isidora Rufete to explore the uneven formation of modern

Introduction

femininity in Spain in the context of the consumerist's debate on female acquisition of fashion. Drawing on the previous studies of the relation among the main character's fondness for dressing stylishly, her defiance of conventional ideals of womanhood, and her attempts to assume agency in the public sphere, this chapter expands on the role that consumerism played in Galdós's presentation of the problematic development of femininity in Spain. It also expands on the implication of the connection between the protagonist's consumption of fashion and the uneasy construction of modern womanhood on the author's stance on Spain's transition to modernity. Isidora's love for finery and the novelist's disapproval of it in the context of nineteenth-century moralists' and conservative intellectuals' arguments against the female consumption of fashion have been discussed at length by scholars. However, Galdós's presentation of the modish protagonist and his sartorial depictions of the supporting female characters (i.e., the Relimpio sisters), show that the author also examined some of the pro-consumerists' points of view as well as the ideas of those who sought to integrate the traits of the modern female shopper into the accepted ideology of domesticity. Weaving the arguments of pro-consumerists with those who attempted to reconcile consumerism with the dominant ideals of femininity into Isidora's portrait enabled Galdós to point to alternatives to the traditional paradigms of womanhood and, at the same time, to call attention to the superficial, and therefore limited, ways in which women could adopt them. Isidora's pursuit of fashion and her ability to develop partially as a subject as well as to participate to a certain extent in the public sphere allowed the novelist not only to dramatize the need to reconfigure the traditional limits of womanhood. It also allowed him to express both his dissatisfaction with the country's slow progress in modernization and his wish for Spain to continue on its path toward becoming a modern nation. Isidora's choice of prostitution powerfully accentuates the lack of *viable* options for women's integration in the urban sphere and points to Galdós's critique of the incompleteness of Spain's modernization. At the same time, the novelist's depiction of his protagonist's vitality and determination to continue to demand at all costs and by all means possible her independence as well as her potential to develop into a full-fledged subject in the future reveal Galdós's support and faith in Spain's capacity for modernization.

Chapter 2, "What Is a Man of Fashion? Manuel Pez and the Dandy in Galdós's *La de Bringas*," explores the author's critique of men's attention to external appearances and shows that the excessive consumption of sartorial goods was not exclusively a women's affair. Impeccably dressed, cynical, and self-absorbed, the male protagonist Manuel Pez shares many of the qualities associated with the popular nineteenth-century narrative figure of the dandy. Thus, he enables Galdós to break down the chimera of the nineteenth-century bourgeois male as an embodiment of sartorial sobriety, uniformity, and propriety, and to cast doubt on the protagonist's adherence to norms of conventional masculinity. Yet, the fancy bureaucrat is not a typical dandy. By endowing this character with attributes that differentiate him from the traditional dandy, that is, by portraying him as a follower of fashion and a dressmaker's dummy, Galdós exposed the bourgeois Spaniards' dependence on foreign ideals of masculinity and denounced their lack of vitality and initiative to move away from the prevalent values and structures of the Ancien Regime. Up-to-date only in his exterior, the dandylike Pez personifies the desire of nineteenth-century Spanish middle-class men (and the Spanish bourgeoisie in general) to look and feel modern without undergoing any substantial changes in their ways of living. Trendy on the outside, but inert and unmanly at the core, the fashionable politician incarnates the illusion of progress and aptly captures the novelist's critical view of the bourgeois Spaniards' superficial idea of modernity.

Chapter 3, "Fashion and Femininity in Pardo Bazán's *Insolación*," focuses on the ways in which the protagonist Asís Taboada's fashionable *toilettes* are implicated in the reinforcement and subversion of the established gender order and in which beauty products, clothing, and accessories function to signal the ambivalent nature of femininity in late-nineteenth-century Spain. Here, my choice of this novel was influenced by the author's vast knowledge of fashion and the expert manipulation of the variety of voguish details in her provocative and, at times, conciliatory presentation of the prevailing gender norms. The use of many of these details echoes the writer's comments on the art of dressing from the time when she was a reporter at the Universal Exhibition in Paris in 1889 and again in 1890. It is in these accounts that one can detect, beneath a light tone in which Pardo Bazán informs readers in Spain about sartorial novelties and new trends in dressing, the author's skillful implication of fashion in the current issues of gender. It is worth observing that Pardo Bazán, like Galdós and Clarín, discussed fashion in the context of class rivalry. Like her colleagues, she too was not indulgent of the bourgeoisie's emulation of the upper strata's dressing styles and the middle-class women's overspending on fashion. In her essay from 1890, "La clase media," for example, Pardo Bazán denounced the emulative habits of the middle class by providing a depiction of a bourgeois *femme* who, despite her modest income, imitates without much success, an affluent aristocrat in her art of dressing:

> Quien viere en el Retiro a dos señoritas, hija la una de un magistrado con diez retoños, y heredera la otra de un título con veinte mil duros de renta, al pronto las tomará por hermanas. El mismo sombrero, el mismo corte de ropa, la misma sombrilla ... Analizad bien ... Los vestidos se parecen en la forma; pero en el uno se ve la tijera del modisto célebre, en el otro el laborioso arreglo hecho a la luz del quinqué de familia. ... El afán de imitar a la aristocracia demuestra en la burguesa falta de independencia y energía. (106)[11]

At the same time, similar to her peers, Pardo Bazán was aware of *la moda* as a fitting medium for highlighting the fissures and contradictions in contemporary constructs of womanhood and manhood in Spain. A keen observer of changes in dressing styles, and a prolific author of articles on fashion in Spain and abroad (Zárate 177–78; 188; 190–91), she frequently availed herself of the symbolic value of sartorial commodities in her narrative to question patriarchal notions of gender. In *Insolación*, details of the female protagonist's external appearance—her grooming activities, hairstyles, and the ways in which she carried herself in her elegant outfits—were constantly engaged in Asís's vacillations between acquiescence and resistance to the typecast role imposed by society on her gender. Conservative and subversive, both subject and object of gaze, a figure to emulate and to condemn, the protagonist continuously confronted and conformed to established notions of femininity. Her portrait, thus, allowed Pardo Bazán not only to bring to light the ambivalent and changing nature of Spanish womanhood but also to experiment with a new model of feminine behavior. In this manner, the novelist was able to accentuate the need to reconfigure traditional ideals of womanhood as a necessary condition for Spain to advance in the process of modernization. Additionally, and more importantly, perhaps, the writer also was able to point out that the successful redefinition of gender norms in Spain would depend on society first comprehending the complexity of a contemporary woman and coming to terms with her continuously evolving, shifting nature.

While challenging the boundaries of traditional womanhood and exploring a new model of feminine conduct was no doubt a bold move on Pardo Bazán's part, equally daring was her endeavor to redefine the limits of conventional femininity by suggesting amendments to the normative masculine role. Chapter 4, "The Sartorial Charm of the Modern Man in Pardo Bazán's *Insolación*," deals with the manner in which the novelist used the language of men's fashion to foreground the incoherencies in the allegedly stable model of late-nineteenth-century bourgeois manhood in Spain. Through the depiction of her protagonist as an individual who is at ease with blending and blurring the conventional and the modern in his dressing styles as well as in his attitude toward the rules of courtship and sexual mores, the novelist ventured to envision an alternative type of bourgeois male. In using the art of dressing to draw the contours of a more desirable model of masculinity in close relation to the unconventional female subject, Pardo Bazán succeeded in emphasizing that finding a new definition for the feminine role, as a part of Spain's modernization, would depend on the successful reshaping of the normative notions of masculinity. The sartorial portrait of Pacheco also constitutes Pardo Bazán's response to the late-nineteenth-century gender anxieties in Spain. By creating a character, who with flair and effortlessness crosses and recrosses the limits of his gender and who, in doing so, not only retains, but also increases his masculine charm, Pardo Bazán downplayed patriarchal fears of modern man as the embodiment of effeminacy and decadence. In this manner, the novelist cajoled her audience to imagine, in a gratifying way, an unconventional image of the bourgeois male and suggested new avenues for the cultural constructions of manhood as a part of the formation of modern Spain.

Chapter 5, "Dressing the New Woman in Picón's *Dulce y sabrosa*," presents yet another writer's riposte via the language of clothing to patriarchal fears related to the late-nineteenth-century crisis of gender and, in particular, the 1890s woman's question in

Introduction

Spain. What is especially intriguing about Jacinto Octavio Picón is that, in contrast to his colleagues, he did not pen a single essay on fashion or feminism. Yet, as his elaborate depictions of female characters show—exquisitely dressed and active in their pursuit of career and personal sovereignty—he was effective in deploying the symbolic value of modish details to voice his unusual perspective on the New Woman. Picón's uncommon stand on the much-debated concept of the New Woman and his manner of expressing it are the reasons I included the analysis of his work in this study. In *Dulce y sabrosa*, the novelist's portrayal of the main character, Cristeta Moreruela, diverges strongly, in many ways, from patriarchal representations of the *femme nouvelle*. Physically beautiful, chic, and in love, the protagonist contradicts the stereotypical images propagated in the conservative press of the New Woman as monstrous, perverse, and incapable of affection. Concurrently, however, Picón's account of Cristeta's attempt to earn a living as an actress points to the author's skepticism of the viability of feminists' claims for economic independence and the quality of work opportunities available for women outside the domestic sphere. Picón's unique (neither entirely feminist nor patriarchal) perspective on the New Woman certainly corroborated his colleagues' position that, as Susan Kirkpatrick put it with respect to Pardo Bazán's writings, "modernising Spain required the modernisation of Spanish women" (146). Through the daring (for his time) sartorial depictions of the protagonist's erotic allure—her luxurious lingerie and sexually charged accessories such as her veil and stockings—the novelist voiced his endorsement of women's right to free themselves from patriarchal concepts of virginity, sexual passivity, and the institution of marriage that held them in a subordinate position to man. At the same time, Picón's veneration of the customary feminine values, evident in his repeated emphasis on the main character's physical beauty, cleanliness, and modesty in dressing, indicates that the writer did not entirely turn his back on the standard ideals of womanhood. By blending, through the language of fashion, the up-to-date and the conventional attributes in his alternative vision of a New Woman, the author toned down the image of her as a threat to the traditional gender hierarchy. In envisioning her as a figure of inspiration for a bourgeois woman to renegotiate her place in society, Picón showed that, like Galdós and Pardo Bazán, he too viewed reconfiguration of the

Introduction

established ideals of femininity as a necessary step in the process of Spain's modernization.

Given that fashion is an enormously complex cultural phenomenon, to exhaust its meaning in the novels under discussion would be beyond the scope of this book. My intention is not to prove that the art of dressing holds the key to explaining *all aspects* of the gender issues addressed by Galdós, Pardo Bazán, and Picón in their narratives. The purpose of this study is, rather, to hone readers' understanding of the ways in which these authors employed references to clothing to enter into a dialogue with the prevailing gender ideology and to express their views artistically on the uneven process of modernization. By conferring central importance to a category that traditionally has received reductive treatment in the analysis of the complex and shifting nature of gender in relation to modernity, I hope to contest the simplistic readings of fashion in Galdós's, Pardo Bazán's, and Picón's novels as trivial, bound primarily to female frivolity and/or class distinction. Because the language of dress is indeed, as Joanne Entwistle and Elizabeth Wilson have claimed (drawing on the observations of cultural historian Fred Davis), "more like music than speech, suggestive and ambiguous rather than bound by the precise grammatical rules" (3) or specific meaning, its significance in these writers' works escapes any absolute conclusions. Since gender and modernity are cultural constructs continually in development (Butler 10–12; Felski 12–15; 21), fashion, identified well before the nineteenth century "as a term for the action or process of making" (Greenblatt 2), is an apropos metaphor for unraveling the complexities of the nineteenth-century Spanish bourgeoisie's efforts to make sense of their existence within the context of modern life.

Chapter One

Fashioning Womanhood and Making Modernity in Galdós's *La desheredada*

"¡El lujo! ¡Cuánto se puede escribir sobre este fenómeno de la vida moderna! ... En Madrid es raro encontrar una mujer que no vaya bien vestida. ... Los establecimientos ... de objetos de gusto ... se han generalizado tanto aquí que es incomprensible cómo viven y cómo encuentran despacho para tantos y tan variados artículos" (124–25), wrote Galdós in his 1893 article, "Vida de sociedad," about the sartorial splendor of the Spanish woman and the development of the modern commercial world in Madrid.[1] In the same year, Galdós also penned a social sketch, "El elegante." In it, while complaining about the lack of variety, discomfort, and drabness of men's clothing, he portrayed Spaniards as consumers of fashion. Additionally, while disapproving of their blind adherence to sartorial etiquette ("se asa en verano con sus chalecos inverosímiles y sus cuellos de cartón y en invierno se muere de frío dentro de los gabanes" [236]), the writer disclosed the importance that the Spanish male attached—whether willingly or not—to the rules of dressing.

The modishness of Madrilenian bourgeois society and the skillfulness with which both women and men deployed the sartorial art to manipulate their outward appearance was no surprise to Galdós at the end of the nineteenth century. As the richness of the voguish details in his portrait of Isidora Rufete in the first of his contemporary novels, *La desheredada* (1881), suggests, the author relied on fashion a decade earlier as an effective medium for addressing major concerns of his time. Yet the sartorial portrayal of Isidora, despite attracting a great deal of scholarly attention (Blanco Carpintero, "El siglo fetichista"; Hoffman, "¿Qué era?"; Martinell), has not been explored fully. Similar to other fashionable female protagonists in Galdós's narratives such as Rosalía Bringas in *La de Bringas* (1884) and Eloísa Raimundo Bueno de Guzmán in *Lo prohibido* (1884–85), Isidora's delight in elegant dresses and accessories mainly has been explained as a cause of her moral downfall and an example of rapacious consumerism motivated by her delusions of grandeur and social ambition (Collins 13–17; Jaffe 36–39; Anderson 57–62).[2]

Undeniably, Isidora's moral downfall and social aspirations have much to do with her extravagant consumption of modish goods and shopping sprees. However, the author's depictions of his protagonist's love for fashion are, at the same time, too recurrent and too meticulous for one to believe that he included them in the novel merely to corroborate the century-old association between female penchant for sartorial luxury and lust or simply to voice his disapproval of the main character's excessive consumerism. Indeed, for some time now, a number of critics have related the protagonist's fondness for dressing stylishly to her resistance to the dominant nineteenth-century ideal of womanhood—the angel of the household—and her endeavors to assert her subjectivity in the public sphere. Fernández Cifuentes examined Isidora's bid to assume agency through her self-construction as a luxurious commodity for sale (308–11). Sieburth emphasized the protagonist's qualities as an artist who fashions her own destiny and subjectivity (27–48). Moreover, Tsuchiya discussed the main character's consumption of finery in the context of her attempts to forge a new space of subjectivity in the public sphere (*Marginal Subjects* 28–45).

I agree with the insights of these scholars who linked Isidora's pursuit of fashion to her defiance of conventional ideals of womanhood and her attempts to assume agency in the public sphere. However, I believe that the connection between the protagonist's consumption of finery and the problematic notion of femininity is worth further exploration as Galdós tied it to issues beyond gender. In what follows, I expand on the role consumerism played in Galdós's presentation of the uneven formation of modern womanhood and on the implication of this link for his stance on Spain's transition to modernity. More specifically, I will demonstrate how the novelist's manners of weaving the arguments of pro-consumerists and those who sought to reconcile consumerism with the dominant ideals of femininity into Isidora's portraits enabled him to point to alternatives to the traditional paradigms of womanhood and, concurrently, to call attention to the superficial and, therefore, limited ways in which women could adopt them. Isidora's ability to develop partially as subject and to participate to a certain extent in the public sphere—as critics have implied or explicitly stated in previous studies—is of particular interest here. Drawing on Celia Amorós's observations that a truly democratic project requires engagement of fully autonomous subjects of both gender (24–27), in this study I reveal how Galdós's use of Isidora's pursuit of fashion to dramatize the need to reconfigure the traditional limits of womanhood relates to the author's position on the country's slow modernization and, simultaneously, to his wish for Spain to become a modern nation.

The nineteenth-century moralists' and conservative intellectuals' arguments against women's consumption of sartorial goods are well documented by scholars. Although female overspending on fashion was a subject of strong criticism already prior to the nineteenth century (Aldaraca, *El Ángel del Hogar* 88–100), it was after the confiscation of ecclesiastical assets in 1836 and again in 1854 that the Spanish clergy and the conservative sector of the bourgeoisie launched a vigorous campaign against women's consumption of finery (Andreu 19–22). In 1869, in "La moralidad en España," the conservative intellectual J. Jimeno Aguis directly related the increasing number of illegitimate children between 1858 and 1864 to the female penchant for modish goods (Andreu 22). In the same year, the economist Antonio María Segovia, in his lecture "Del lujo," linked women's proclivity for sartorial ostentation to illness by referring to it in terms of fever and infection (Jagoe 88). Additionally, in 1875, Pope Pius IX, in his encyclical "Concerning Women and Luxury," warned that women's excessive spending lead to economic disorder and idleness and was considered, therefore, a sin (Aldaraca, *El Ángel del Hogar* 102).

Of course, since all of the disastrous consequences of the female love of luxury addressed in the writings by the aforementioned moralists—illegitimate sexual activities, idleness, economic disorder, and disease—are dutifully recorded in Isidora's story, to some critics the portrait of Galdós's protagonist fits like a glove the classic anti-consumerist example of a fallen woman. "No le gusta trabajar, no hace más que emperifollarse … y lavarse" (186), doña Laura complains to her husband about Isidora's laziness and the amount of water that the young woman spends on her baths. Later, the narrator also confirms that taking care of her *toilette* and her out-of-wedlock son's external appearance is how the protagonist fills her idle hours: "Entre bañarse, peinarse, vestir y arreglar a *Riquín,* se le iba la mañana. Por la tarde … solía matar el fastidio en las iglesias" (317). The economic disorder ("¿En qué había gastado? ... no lo sabía" [243]) is a result of Isidora's overbuying of luxuries: "En perfumería había adquirido lo bastante para tres años" (243). In addition, by the main character's own admission, it is "este defecto de volverme loca con el lujo" (489), in other words, her incurable addiction to finery that engages her in the illegitimate sexual activities with men who are willing and able to pay her bills.

However, Galdós's sartorial presentation of Isidora and the world around her suggests more than meets the eye. As Kathleen E. Davis has claimed, "concentration on the works of the anti-consumerists has tended to obscure the fact that there was social *debate* about the ethics of consumerism, both in journalism and in fiction" (12–13; Davis's italics) and that "fashion writers, as well as popular and literary authors, answered the charges of anti-consumerists by attempting to reconcile consumer values with domesticity" (13). In support of her argument, Davis examines the pro-consumerists' logic as outlined during the late 1880s and 1890s in articles by the Spanish fashion critic Blanca Valmont and the echoing of this reasoning in Galdós's *Lo prohibido*.

Yet voices of those who expressed a viewpoint about consumer values different from the common anti-materialist and created an image of an acquisitive female other than that of a fallen woman marked their presence (at least in nonfiction works) prior to the last two decades of the nineteenth century (Valis, *The Culture* 141–49). As for Galdós's narratives, the author examined different types of femininity that emerged in the context of the debate of female consumption of fashion as presented not only from the perspective of the anti-consumerists, but also from the standpoint of their opponents and those who sought to reconcile modern consumer values with domestic ideology already in *La desheredada*. As early as the first part of the novel, in his account of Isidora's observations on the elegance of the Madrilenian crowd, the narrator laid out some of the pro-consumerists' arguments and characteristics of a modern, urbane type of woman that was promoted in their discourse. Consider the description of Isidora's veneration of the sophisticatedly attired couples in El Retiro during her tour with Miquis.

> Aquella naturaleza ... despertaba en su ... espíritu instintos ... de candoroso salvajismo. Pero ... comprendió que aquello era un campo urbano ... Por allí andaban damas y caballeros ... con guantes, sombrilla ... se acostumbró ... a considerar el Retiro ... como una ... adaptación de la naturaleza a la cultura; comprendió que el hombre que ha domesticado a las bestias, ha sabido también civilizar al bosque. ... Para otra vez ... traeré yo también mis guantes y mi sombrilla. (118)

Underlying the protagonist's admiration is the idea (and at the same time one of the major pro-consumerist arguments in the debate) that luxury is "alma del progreso y de la civilización" (1), as Fernando Garrido put it in his essay, "El lujo," published in 1857 in *El Nuevo Pensil de Iberia*.[3] What enraptures Isidora, who had arrived only a few days before in the capital from La Mancha, is the cultured appearance of El Retiro crowd and the chic of the urban, modern woman who exhibits, as she was encouraged to do in the pro-consumerists' discourse, her fashionable accouterments. "[Q]ue ostentáis diamantes, que os cubrís de encajes, pisáis terciopelo y arrastráis sedas ... Alzad la voz, y decidles ... que ya es tarde para contener vuestra vanidad excitada ... Si la virtud os condena, ¡qué importa!; la civilización os absuelve" (108), wrote social commentator José Selgas in his 1871 article "El lujo de las mujeres."

That Isidora lays her eyes precisely on the gloves and parasol is, of course, scarcely a coincidence here. Although, as the contemporary fashion historian Pena González noted, already in the early decades of the nineteenth century both items constituted "accesorio imprescindible de señorita cuya principal función era la de preservar la tez del bronceado" ("Indumentaria" 101), as time moved on, these posh accessories became the hallmarks of cultural progress and sophistication. More than any other articles of fashion, they attested to the celebration of female taste and beauty in the urban space and emphasized women's participation, however limited, in public life. "Se llevan puestos los guantes para salir a la calle, para el paseo, la iglesia, el jardín y el teatro ... los guantes deben usarse siempre, y por todos los que frecuentan el mundo social" (279–80), counseled well-known Catalonian journalist and playwright Alfredo Pallardó writing under the pseudonym of Viscountess Bestard de la Torre in *La elegancia en el trato social: Reglas de etiqueta y cortesanía en todos los actos de la vida* (1898).[4]

Chapter One

Additionally, the narrator's description of Isidora's excitement over the mind-boggling variety of articles of clothing, styles, and colors displayed by the smartly dressed throng in the Castellana correlates with the pro-consumerists' stance that the proliferation of goods stimulated female creativity and with the image of a fashionable, modern woman conversant in employing sartorial items as a means of artistic self-expression.

> Los bustos de las damas ... los variados matices de las sombrillas, las libreas, las pieles, producían ante su vista un efecto igual al que en cualquiera de nosotros produciría la contemplación de un magnífico fresco ... —¡Qué variedad de sombreros! ¡Mira éste, mira aquél ... ! ... (134–35)

Commenting on this scene, Collin McKinney points to Isidora's failure to note "lo que todo el mundo ve" (133) and what Miquis observes in the Castellana spectacle, namely, the parade of social aspirants. While "Miquis identifies them as 'cursi'" (60), wrote McKinney, "Isidora, on the other hand, accepts the spectacle at face value"(60). Yet the main character's ignorance is not all that this scene reveals. Given the statement "Isidora, para quien aquel espectáculo, además de ser enteramente nuevo, tenía particulares seducciones, vio algo más de lo que vemos todos" (133), which points to the disparity in perspectives and, more importantly, as the use of the first person plural of the verb *ver* in conjunction with the word *todos* implies, to the limitation of others' vision (besides that of the protagonist), it remains questionable whether the main character, indeed, is the only one who takes the Castellana spectacle at face value.[5] While Isidora refuses to acknowledge what Miquis describes as "trampas, fanatismo, ignorancia, presunción" (135) of the passing society, the young doctor proves to be equally unwilling and/or unable to notice anything else beyond the tackiness, vanity, and social ambition of the richly adorned crowd.

There is no doubt that social aspiration and vanity are at the heart of the narrator's depiction of Isidora's enthrallment with the sartorial splendor in this scene. After all, at this point, the young woman firmly believes herself to be part of the *marquesa* de Aransis's family. However, the narrator's meticulous account of pattern, fabrics, and colors and his repeated references to Isidora's astonishment and excitement over the originality of items foreground the idea that there is something more than mere social distinction that the protagonist associates with the modish crowd. By drawing attention to the variety of fashionable goods (underscored through the use of the demonstrative pronouns *éste* and *aquél*) and Isidora's amazement with them (reinforced through the presence of imperatives), the narrator takes pains to show that she is equally, if not more, awestruck by the wide assortment of stylish *toilettes*. "Isidora no volvía de su asombro"; "sus ojos maravillados"; "¡Vaya un vestidito!" (133; 134; 135). What the main character admires, thus, parallel to class distinction, are the multiple and creative manners in which a bourgeois woman could arrange her look outside her domestic walls. She is flabbergasted, in other words, by the agency and autonomy that the richness of fashionable commodities and the plethora of styles could render a woman (if only in limited ways) in terms of her artistic self-expression in the public space.

Lastly, there is the pro-consumerist argument of democratization of fashion that Galdós explores in Isidora's story. Already in 1852, an anonymous writer for *El mensajero de las modas* commented that dressing *à la mode* was no longer an exclusive privilege of upper-class ladies, but a prerogative of all women in Spain. "En otro tiempo solo inspiraba la moda sus caprichos a las clases elevadas de la sociedad ... Al presente puede asegurarse que ha invadido todo el dominio social. ... la gracia y el lujo pertenece hoy por derecho de conquista a todas las mujeres" (qtd. in Pena González, *Traje* 47). As the century progressed and articles of clothing became mass-produced, pro-consumerists further developed their claim that fashion was now available to all by insisting that dressing stylishly was a matter of elegance (which they equated, paradoxically like their opponents, with simplicity) and not opulence. Some of them went as far in their argument as to contend that a woman's sense of style and her talent for dressing could alone qualify her to aspire to move in the highest circles of society (K. E. Davis 56; 67–68).[6]

The resonance of this logic, as well as the skepticism toward it, is easily detectable in Isidora's story. At the end of the first part of the novel, the protagonist's uncle wrote: "Por más que aseguren que esta igualdad se ha iniciado ya en ... el vestido ... a mí no me entra eso. ... ¿Los salones de la aristocracia se abren a todo el mundo ... ? A otro perro con ese hueso" (283). As for Isidora, she shares her uncle's elitist views as long as she believes in her claim to be part of the *marquesa* de Aransis family. However, as winning

Chapter One

her lawsuit and gaining admittance to society via the traditional route—through noble lineage and wealth—becomes increasingly problematic, she turns to the pro-consumerist idea of equality.

> Contemplóse en el gran espejo, embelesada de su hermosura. … Isidora encontraba mundos de poesía en aquella reproducción de sí misma. ¡Qué *diría* la sociedad si pudiera gozar de tal imagen! ¡Cómo la *admirarían*, y con qué entusiasmo habían de celebrarla las lenguas de la fama! … Ella era noble por su nacimiento, y si no lo fuera, *bastaría* a darle la ejecutoria su gran belleza, su figura, sus gustos delicados, sus simpatías por toda cosa elegante y superior. (401; my italics)

One could attribute the presence of verbs in the conditional form in this excerpt to the narrator's skeptical attitude toward Isidora's wishful thinking that her sophisticated taste in dressing and grace alone would qualify her to become, as pro-consumerists implied, and as was the case of the Modern Parisian woman, "the new 'aristocrat' in a bourgeois capitalist world" (Steele, *Paris* 75). However, the use of the conditional, particularly in combination with reference to France through the setting of this scene—Madame Eponina's shop—suggests more than the narrator's distance from sharing the protagonist's personal hopes. "Pues vete a París. Allí encontrarás tu puesto. … Aquí no las gastamos de tanto lujo como tú. … Aquí te degradarás demasiado" (404), Miquis tells Isidora during their conversation in the French dressmaker's establishment. In France, as Steele wrote, drawing on Balzac's essay "La Femme comme il faut" (1839), the ideal of the Modern Parisian "embraced women across the social spectrum" (*Paris* 75) and "was a representative of both Society and modern society" (*Paris* 75). In Spain, however, the situation was different. While even prior to the Revolution of 1868, as Benedetto Croce and David Ringrose have shown, the country "was making meaningful progress toward a modern economy, society, and standard of living" (Ringrose 64), contradictions between tradition and modernity still persisted in various aspects of life.[7] Consequently, it was more problematic for a Spanish bourgeois woman to develop fully into a figure similar to the "Parisienne" than it was for a middle-class female in Madame Eponina's homeland. Hence, this is what Galdós appears to convey through his narrator's skeptical attitude and his allusion to France in this scene and in his exploration of the characteristics of the modern urban type of woman promoted in the pro-consumerist discourse in general. Although the progressive type of femininity endorsed by the pro-consumerists was appealing to bourgeois women in Spain, in reality, this ideal was difficult, if not impossible, for most of these women to embrace.

If Spanish middle-class women could not adopt all of the traits of modern consumers of fashion, could they assimilate some of the Modern Parisienne's enticing features? In other words, was it possible to weave some of the pro-consumerist values into the ideology of domesticity? Galdós seems to answer this question through the sartorial portraits of the secondary female personages in the novel. Take, for example, the following description of the Relimpio daughters:

> Su pobreza les vedaba ciertamente el lujo; pero como es ley que todas las clases de la sociedad ... vistan de la misma manera, y como hay un verdadero delirio en los pequeños por imitar el modo de presentarse de los grandes ... las de Relimpio se emperifollaban tan bien con recortes, desechos, pingos y cosas viejas rejuvenecidas, que más de una vez dieron chasco a los poco versados en fisonomías y tipos matritenses. ... Mas a fuerza de trabajar, de desvelos y de casi inverosímiles economías, lograron vestirse y calzarse ambas de la misma manera, y aun tener sendos sombreros de moda, arreglados por ellas ... con despojos y reliquias de otros sombreros. (188–89)

Given the blatant criticism of the petite bourgeoisie's penchant for imitation, which the narrator interjects in his depiction of the Relimpio sisters (as if to say that this is the major reason for including the sartorial portrayal of these characters in the novel), it is tempting to interpret this passage as merely an example of *cursilería* in the novel. There is, after all, Isidora's disdainful assessment of her cousins' appearance ("Estas pobres cursis" [188]) that precedes the narrator's depiction of them. However, even if the narrator placed Isidora's comment ahead of his portrait of the Relimpio daughters in order to guide the reader's opinion of them, is *cursilería* all that this detailed excerpt reveals? In other words, if the narrator, indeed, availed himself of the description of Emilia and Leonor Relimpio mainly to criticize the middle class's tackiness, why did he bother to place so much emphasis on these young women's hard work and efforts to look chic *within their economic means?*

Scholars have documented the conservative women writers' (Aldaraca, *El Ángel del Hogar* 113–17) and the pro-consumerists'

Chapter One

(K. E. Davis 71–74) endeavors to reconcile the modern consumer values with domestic ideology. Although there are differences in reasons for which each group attempted to mold the female consumption of finery into the discourse of domesticity, both sides shared the opinion that all women should keep up with fashion. Additionally, while they differed as to suggestions regarding the ways in which individuals of limited income could imitate fashion, both maintained that dressing smartly was an activity open to all women as long as they kept with "the formula of elegance *by means* of economy" (Aldaraca, *El Ángel del Hogar* 116; Aldaraca's italics).

In 1878, in her conduct manual *Mujer en nuestros días*, María del Pilar Sinués de Marco, for instance, offered as a solution to less affluent readers to imitate at home "los elegantes modelos que ya en figurines iluminados, ya en grabados en negro, dan con profusión los periódicos de modas" (145). By encouraging women to make their own wardrobe instead of relying on a dressmaker, that is, by pointing out to her audience the possibility of following the latest fad while keeping low the cost of dressing *à la mode*, Sinués de Marco demonstrated how fashion could be a virtue within the domestic ideology:

> Muy pocos años hace … que oíamos decir á las señoritas: —Yo no sé hacer otra cosa que dibujar y tocar el piano: todos mis vestidos los hace la modista; no tomo la aguja para nada. Hoy es ridículo decir esto, y más todavía hacerlo. … Se sabe … que muchas … señoras han comprometido sériamente su fortuna por las cuentas de sus modistas; sin embargo … conocemos algunas que … han encontrado un privilegio para vestir con elegancia, sin arruinarse por eso. ¿Y sabeis cómo? Acostumbrándose á cortar por sí mismas sus trajes … á tomar ellas mismas parte en su confeccion. (141–42)

Writing two decades later, Valmont presented women of scarce financial resources with similar advice by directing their attention to the advances in the clothing industry and the opportunity to purchase (instead of making at home) reasonably priced imitations of costly fabrics, gemstones, feathers, and other goods. She too ventured to integrate consumerism into the accepted ideology of domesticity in that she promoted the idea of looking stylish within one's economic means and by making her audience believe that wearing inexpensive imitation items would produce the same effect as donning the pricey originals.

> Respondiendo a esta transformación que lentamente ha venido operándose en nuestra indumentaria, las telas se han abaratado considerablemente ... las imitaciones se hacen tan bien que se confunden con sus originales ... Además, la pedrería, las plumas, los encajes y cuanto constituye el adorno de una dama, se falsifican de tal manera que sólo despues de una larga y minuciosa comprobación, puede distinguirse lo que es legítimo de lo que no lo es. (qtd. in K. E. Davis 57)

However, how viable were these recommendations, Galdós appears to ask through his portrait of the Relimpio daughters and through his depiction of the protagonist in Chapter 13 (not by chance entitled "¡Cursilona!")? How much pleasure did women draw from their looks, women like the Relimpio sisters and Isidora herself who followed such advice? The irony that stems from the discrepancy between the Relimpios' efforts to look elegant and the pitiful results that their sartorial presentation effected leaves little doubt regarding Galdós's position on these new and improved angels of domesticity who supposedly could do wonders with a needle in their hands and whose image was promoted heavily by conservative authors and, to some extent, in the writings of the pro-consumerists. As the narrator highlights with respect to the Relimpio daughters, no one, except "los poco versados en fisonomías y tipos matritenses" (188), could be misled by their cheap improvisations. The author further reinforces his position in describing Isidora's embarrassment by the shabbiness of her wardrobe during the visit to Joaquín Pez's house. Through this scene, he shows that not even the main character—so superior to her cousins in matters of elegance in dressing—was able to impress her admirer. Despite spending "dos horas arreglándose para disimular su mala facha" (234), and despite arriving "compuesta con galana sencillez, respirando aseo y coquetería" (234), she feels inferior to everyone else around her. This is because, as Galdós's narrator states straightforwardly (and, as if responding to the conservative authors' praises of the domestic angel's cleanliness, simplicity, and thrift), "todo el aseo del mundo, toda la gracia y sencillez no podían disimular la fea catadura del descolorido traje, ni menos ... la desgraciadísima vejez y mucho uso de las botas, que no sólo estaban usadas y viejas, sino ¡rotas!" (234).

It bears noting that the recommendation to dress within one's means was not necessarily an attempt on Sinués de Marco's part to keep middle-class women in their place. As Íñigo Sánchez Llama's study shows, the priority in Sinués de Marco's, Grassi de Cuenca's, and Sáez de Melgar's writings was to prepare women to deal with the uncertainties of the modern era and to adapt to changes in the economic and social structures brought by evolving capitalism (106–07; 144–50). Sinués de Marco and her colleagues endorsed many advanced ideas (for their time) about women's education, work, and leisure (Sánchez Llama 174–80). Nevertheless, while keeping up with fashion in moderation might have been an adequate response to the female penchant for finery in decades prior to the 1880s, as the century moved on, consumerism, Galdós seems to say in *La desheredada*, became far too dynamic and far too entrenched in the life of Spanish women to be absorbed into the traditional ideals of femininity.

Consider the manner in which Galdós's narrator depicts Isidora's reaction to the modish goods on display in Chapter 7, in the first part of the novel. "Empezó a ver escaparates … Ésta era su delicia mayor … y origen de vivísimos apetitos … devoraba con sus ojos las infinitas variedades y formas del lujo y de la moda" (172). One can certainly accept Tsuchiya's interpretation that this passage anticipates the protagonist's prostitution. As Tsuchiya reminded us, nineteenth-century novelists frequently used eating to link female desire for consumption with erotic desire (*Marginal Subjects* 34). Yet the correlation between physiological needs such as eating and the female urge to acquire novelties could also be the author's way of making his audience aware that pursuing fashion in late-nineteenth-century Spain became an activity that could no longer be mediated by traditional arguments. By placing the need to consume finery on par with the most indispensable human function—satisfying hunger—the narrator dramatized the significance that acquisition of goods gained in a woman's existence, its implication in matters larger than Isidora's moral flaws, and, indirectly, the necessity to find a more appropriate way for addressing it in the context of modern life.

Scholars have related, as mentioned earlier, the main character's acquisitive appetite and manner of dressing to her resistance to the established notions of femininity and her attempts to assume agency outside domestic walls. Overall, it is not only through the depictions of the act of consumption, but also through the symbolic value of Isidora's wardrobe, that Galdós's narrator brings these matters to light. Consider, for instance, the meaning of the protagonist's black dress and boots at the beginning of Chapter 4. "Aquel día estrenaba unas botas. ¡Qué bonitas eran y qué bien le sentaban! ... Púsose su vestidillo negro ... y volvió a mirarse las botitas" (115). Chad Wright, in his analysis of another Galdosian female protagonist, Amparo Sánchez Emperador in *Tormento* (1884), explained that a black dress was associated in nineteenth-century Spain with both a wedding gown and a death shroud. Although Isidora's circumstances are different from those of Amparo, who by putting on the black dress attempts literally "to kill her social self and goes through a type of resurrection to a new, freer life" (Wright 33), the black gown in *La desheredada* reinforces the main character's desire to renounce symbolically her life as a domestic angel. Also as a wedding dress, Isidora's black gown speaks her defiance of the conventional ideal of womanhood. According to an anonymous writer's essay from 1861 in *La Moda Elegante*, as a wedding dress, a black gown was a "simbolo ... de un rito ... parecido al luto: la novia moría al mundo de las solteras" (qtd. in Perinat and Marrades 144–45). Therefore, in the context of Isidora's story, her outfit stands for her wish to "die socially" to the world of the unmarried Relimpio sisters whose image of hard-working, honest, and humble young women the protagonist considers old-fashioned and unappealing.[8] Similarly, the main character's quest for agency within the modern consumer culture is well articulated through the symbolic meaning of her boots. As if drawing on the erotic connotation (Litvak 123–24; Longares 36), and the instinct for autonomy associated in nineteenth-century Spain with women's footwear (Charnon-Deutsch, *Gender* 152), the narrator prefigures—via his emphasis on Isidora's boots and the verb *estrenar* in conjunction with them—the manner in which she will negotiate her place in the public sphere.[9]

However, Isidora's pursuit of fashion allows her to assert her independence only in limited ways. As critics have noted, through the consumption and manipulation of sartorial goods the main character is able to enhance her persona only in the realm of self-created fiction (Sieburth 37) or by forging subjective—not real—spaces of desire (Tsuchiya, *Marginal Subjects* 57). In becoming a public woman, her agency as a seller is uncertain (Labanyi 115–17). For whether she will promote herself as a luxurious or ordinary commodity (Fernández Cifuentes 311), as a prostitute, she will assume mostly the role of an object for sale.

Of course, one could view the protagonist's claims for autonomy via consumption of fashion mainly as a gender matter. After all, through Isidora's decision to gain access (however limited) to the public sphere in exchange for her body, Galdós denounces the lack of *viable* options for women—an appropriate education and career that would win them financial autonomy—to reshape the limits of their gender and assert their independence outside domestic walls. However, thinking of the ways in which feminism exposes flaws and contradictions of modernity, which as "proyecto ilustrado entendido como la emancipación del sujeto racional" (Amorós 320) denied women's right to assert their subjectivity and to enter the public sphere, it appears that Galdós implicated Isidora's struggle for autonomy in issues larger than gender.

In her reconstruction of different aspects and stages of development of what she calls "sujeto de la modernidad" (30), Celia Amorós describes the post–French Revolution reality as a series of pacts among men. While the revolution made it possible to shatter the foundations of the Ancien Regime and to recognize most men as individuals, rational subjects, and citizens, it did very little in terms of improving the situation of women. "Los hechos han probado que los hombres tenían o creían tener intereses muy diferentes de los de las mujeres, puesto que en todos lados han hecho contra ellas leyes opresivas o al menos establecido entre los dos sexos una gran desigualdad" (170), wrote Amorós, quoting Condorcet. As a consequence, "ha aflorado ... en las mujeres la conciencia de 'Tercer Estado dentro del Tercer Estado,' y de que ... sus intereses no son los mismos ni siquiera que los de los varones de sus clases" (Amorós 170). In denying women's right to define their own individuality and, hence, their subjectivity, men succeeded, in sum, in preserving the status quo with respect to the opposite sex. While keeping women as transactional objects among themselves (among males), men effectively excluded the fairer sex from taking part in the construction of modern society and from calling for agency in the public sphere (Amorós 170–72).

It is true that Amorós centers her discussion on women's claims for independence and the link between these requests and paradoxes of modernity in cultural contexts different from Galdós's Spain. Nonetheless, her observations, particularly in light of Fourier's thought that "el cambio de una época histórica puede determinarse siempre por la actitud de progreso de la mujer ante la libertad" (qtd. in Amorós 112), are of particular interest here. They are illuminating with respect to the use that Galdós made of Isidora's struggle for subjectivity via fashion to convey his views on the progress of modernization in Spain. Certainly, changes in political and socioeconomic structures in post-revolution France were different from the outcomes of the 1868 September revolution and the First Republic in Spain. However, as in the case of the French Revolution, the 1868 uprising and the First Republic changed very little, as scholars have shown (Scanlon 21–49; 58–89; Scott 4–5; 16–17) and as Galdós had demonstrated in his novel, with regard to women's *real* opportunities for education, employment, and their access to the public sphere.

Although, as Scott puts it, "Isidora has been educated to believe that she is a lady and behaves accordingly" (57), it should be recognized that the first time the protagonist mentions to Miquis her desire to enhance *even slightly* her knowledge ("deseo aprender algo más" [122]; "un poquito, una idea de todo" [124]), her request is immediately declined. By undermining her confidence in her capacity to learn, by calling her, if only jokingly, "tonta ... un pozo de ignorancia" (122), and by trying to convince her that her physical beauty and ability to take care of a household are more appealing to him than her interest in learning ("Vidita, no te me hagas sabia. El mayor encanto de la mujer es la ignorancia" [124]), Miquis reverberates the common prejudice against the attempts to improve women's education in late-nineteenth-century Spain. Similarly, Isidora's thoughts to employ her good taste in dressing and to sew for a living are doomed to failure. Although there are indications on the narrator's part that it is the protagonist's idleness and lofty thoughts that keep her away from trying to set up her own place to sew, it is not merely the hard working conditions and lack of respect for women in this profession that stop Isidora from choosing this path. She refuses to tie herself to the sewing machine because, as she can see from the Relimpios' example, the low wages that she would earn for her labor would not afford her financial freedom, but instead, force her into perpetual slavery.[10]

Yet, the defects of the social system in terms of education and career opportunities for women seem to be only in part to blame for the slow progress of modernization. The author's emphasis on Isidora's efforts to make her mark through her innovative toilettes, her individuality and subjectivity and society's refusal to acknowledge it (as the last scene of the main character's disappearing in a crowd would imply), is meaningful for another reason. By portraying Isidora, who despite her efforts to retain her autonomy remains throughout the novel mainly in the role of an object of sexual desire, Galdós pointed to the deficiency in the inner nature of Spain's modernization. Through his depictions of the protagonist as a mistress and as a future prostitute, the author brought to light the inflexibility of Spanish society's way of thinking of a woman in spaces and relations to men other than those already assigned to her by patriarchal conventions.

Isidora's decision to plunge into the life of a prostitute as the only way to enter the public sphere seems to leave hardly any doubt about Galdós's position on the effects that failure to provide women with new—real—spaces of subjectivity had on Spain's uneven transition to modernity. However, if indeed, as Amorós put it, "no se reconstruye el pasado sino en función de lo que en el presente se quiere construir" (84), we may assume that the account of Isidora's struggle to assert her agency and the lack of closure in her story relate to Galdós's wish for Spain as a modern nation. Of course, given Isidora's past as a kept woman and her future as a prostitute, it is patent that the writer did not imply that she would be able to free herself from the status of an object. Concurrently, however, the emphasis on Isidora's consumption of fashion via which she claims her autonomy shows that Galdós recognized, as Toril Moi contends, drawing on Simone de Beauvoir's *The Second Sex* (1949), "the body alone does not define a woman" (71). In bringing forward Isidora's love for dressing stylishly, which reinforces the notion of her (in de Beauvoir's terms) as continuously in the process of making herself, instead of being a fixed reality (Moi 62–63), Galdós highlighted the way in which she constantly engages her adorned body to reinterpret her presence in the world and to assume, in this manner, her subjectivity. This is not to say that the constant reinterpretation that Galdós captured so well in his character's manipulation of sartorial goods and styles could alone gain Isidora full autonomy. However, the lack of closure in Isidora's story and the author's account of her in the final chapter "as an open-ended becoming" (Moi 83) shows that Galdós was not too quick to dismiss her claims for agency in the future. Considering that during the time that the writer examined in retrospect, namely, the six years following the Revolution of 1868, no radical changes took place regarding women's position in society, it is natural that Isidora developed her subjectivity only in limited ways. However, even if the emphasis on this limited agency reflects undoubtedly Galdós's disappointment with the incompleteness of Spanish modernization, his depiction of his protagonist's vitality and determination in the last chapter to continue to demand at all costs and by all means possible her independence, reveals the author's wish for Spain to proceed on its path toward becoming a modern nation.

Isidora's choice of prostitution over the honorable life of a domestic angel surely points to Galdós's dramatization of the need to reconfigure the traditional limits of womanhood in Spain. However, given the skepticism and pity that his narrator deliberately evokes in readers through the description of the protagonist's daydreaming to transcend her condition by means of her sartorial beauty and perseverance alone, one cannot help but notice that the author availed himself of Isidora's choice to pass on a larger message. It is no coincidence that Galdós's narrator mentions the excitement in the conversation between Isidora and a woman from a brothel over the new outfits in the final chapter. Precisely because the strategy to deploy the "frivolous" art of fashion to negotiate her price and place on the market could not possibly inspire trust in the effectiveness of Isidora's venture, the likely skepticism toward the protagonist provided Galdós with a protective cover to mark the protagonist's struggle to achieve her selfhood as a step forward toward Spain's modernization. Ahead of his era in recognizing that true democracy requires an engagement of fully independent subjects of both genders (Amorós 24–25), Galdós used the presumption that Isidora's endeavor to assert her autonomy would fail to indicate that her freedom would not be given. It will not occur naturally nor will it happen through a one-time decision or choice she makes. Instead, the protagonist, and by extension all women, must negotiate their independence persistently and over an extensive stretch of time.

Chapter One

It bears noting that whatever the consequences of Isidora's action in the last chapter might be, it is clear that she has a chance to become a full-fledged subject only outside society's current prescriptive gender role. At present, however, given the societal impediments that deny her autonomy, she is, like modernity itself, a partially developed project, a subject in the process of becoming, a prospect of that which is yet to come. Thus far, it is in her potential subjectivity—and not the immediate results—that Galdós deposited his hopes for the future. In other words, it is in the process of Isidora's self-realization, in which Galdós anticipated failures and obstacles to overcome, but from which it was impossible (as the conversation with Relimpio at the end reveals) to steer his protagonist away by means of traditional arguments, that we can sense the author's support and faith in Spain's capacity for modernization.

In conclusion, as one can see, there is much more at stake in Galdós's presentation of the protagonist's consumption of fashion than a critique of female vanity. In linking Isidora's fondness for dressing stylishly to her defiance of traditional ideals of womanhood and her attempts to assert her independence in the public sphere, Galdós not only accentuated the need to redefine the dominant constructs of femininity. He also used the partially developed feminine subjectivity and women's limitations to access the public sphere to express both his dissatisfaction with the incompleteness of Spain's modernization and his desire for a better future. Certainly, Isidora's pursuit of fashion is not all-encompassing in terms of Galdós's position on Spain's struggle for transformation to modernity. Although granting women the status of full-fledged subjects and placing them inside, rather than outside, of spaces valorized by the dominant culture were essential for the construction of modern society, these were not the only conditions required for Spain's successful transition to modernity. It is true that when Amorós states that "sin sujetos autónomos, responsables, reflexivos y críticos, el proyecto democrático carecería de sentido" (25) she refers mainly to women, since it is the first element—autonomy—that women lacked during the periods under discussion. However, we may not assume that being a male autonomous subject automatically implied the presence of the three other factors that Amorós lists in her comment. If read with a careful eye Galdós's images of Isidora's frenzy for sartorial goods, we may notice, in fact, that these depictions are connected, in one way or another, to the male pursuit of elegance. Numerous references to men's adherence to sartorial etiquette and fondness for dressing smartly show that Galdós did not overlook male consumerism as a fertile ground for exploring the crisis of masculinity and its consequences for Spain's incorporation into modernity. While images of fashion-consuming men, such as Joaquín Pez, Melchior Relimpio, or even Miquis later in his career, are not scant in *La desheredada*, it is in Galdós's later novel, *La de Bringas*, that the writer linked more explicitly the male pursuit of elegance to the problematic notion of masculinity.[11] As we shall see in the elaborated portrait of Manuel Pez in the following chapter, by linking the dandylike image of this character to the imitation of foreign style of dressing and foreign ideals of manhood, Galdós hardly presented the bourgeois male as a responsible, critical, or reflexive subject. Instead, once again, the author availed himself of his protagonist's love for dressing trendy to engage in dialogue with the dominant gender discourse and to voice in this way his position on the subject of modernity.

Chapter Two

What Is a Man of Fashion? Manuel Pez and the Dandy in Galdós's *La de Bringas*

"No he visto nunca en novelas españolas un elegante tan bien hecho como el don Alvaro de Mesía. Es completo, tipo admirable en su ligereza y corrupción provinciana. Pues y el marquesito de Vegallana también es hermosísimo" wrote Galdós on April 6, 1885, in a letter to Leopoldo Alas (Clarín) about the creation of two male characters in *La Regenta* (1885) (qtd. in Ortiz 92). However, while Galdós was marveling at Clarín's protagonists, he himself had already contributed to the gallery of fictional dandies and *señoritos* in the nineteenth-century Spanish novel. Several of Galdós's characters captured the essence of the *señorito*, such as Joaquinito Pez in *La desheredada* (1881) and José María Bueno de Guzmán in *Lo prohibido* (1885).[1] In 1884, the author added a new dimension to Manuel Pez, whom he had introduced as an influential politician and as Joaquinito Pez's father in *La desheredada*. Impeccably dressed, cynical, and self-absorbed, Pez in *La de Bringas* shares many of the attributes of the dandy, so popular in the nineteenth-century narrative. Yet, Galdós's Pez is not a conventional dandy. The object of the present study is to show in what ways Manuel Pez resembles and, simultaneously, differs from the traditional dandy as well as what the image of this character reveals about Galdós's perception of the nineteenth-century Spanish bourgeois man. In particular, this study examines the extent to which Galdós questions the prevailing notions of bourgeois masculinity via his dandylike portrait of Pez and the ways in which the novelist links his protagonist's fashionable image and uncertain manhood to Spain's struggle for incorporation into modernity.

The word *dandy* is of ambiguous origin. According to Ellen Moers, "[d]ictionaries trace it back no farther than the seventeen-eighties, as a term of vague significance in Scottish border songs, and offer as a source merely the local diminutive for Andrew (or

Chapter Two

the English "Jack-a-Dandy")" (11). Earlier than that, the word *dandy* appeared in the oldest stanzas of "Yankee Doodle" written by an anonymous Englishman and sung throughout the American colonies in the 1770s to ridicule the poorly dressed American troops. As a social phenomenon, dandyism in England originated during George IV's reign and was imported to France after the fall of Napoleon. It started with Beau Brummell, who with his austere, impeccably fitting clothing, refined *toilette*, and theatrical demeanor revolutionized the appearance of the aristocracy in England and the *manière d'être* of bourgeois men in Europe for the rest of the century.

Deeply connected to modernity and its cultural expressions in fashion, urbanization, and the cult of self, dandyism has provided a rich ground for observing changes in modern life. To Baudelaire, for example, dandyism was a manifestation of modern individualism, "the burning need to create for oneself a personal originality" (27). For Benjamin and Kracauer, dandies were significant components in the landscape of modern city boulevards.[2] Most recently, Rhonda Garelick has argued that the ideals of dandyism are similar to those of fashion because "[b]oth depend upon phases of newness, foreignness, surprise and scandal. Both concern the aesthetics of performance; both strive to grasp the present, existing only in an unnarratable 'now'" (59). However, in addition to being the focus of "las obras teóricas y los ensayos en que el tema se analiza y se interpreta ... el dandysmo," Luis Antonio de Villena reminds us, "es sujeto y tema de la literatura" (33).

Although the catalog of fictional dandies in the Spanish narrative appears to be somewhat shorter than the list of literary dandies in French and English novels, this does not mean, of course, that nineteenth-century Spanish authors did not experiment with dandyism (Ortiz 61–67). Mariano José de Larra, for instance, was fascinated with the figure of the dandy (Umbral 83–85; Heath 22–29). In "El castellano viejo" (1832), Larra displays himself as a dandy poised tensely in his frock coat, "limpísima camisa ... y ... pantalón color de perla" (317). In "La Nochebuena de 1836" (1836), the essayist again presents himself as a man who is conscious of his clothing: "frac elegante ... media de seda, y ... chaleco de tisú de oro" (556) on one hand, and of his bitter self-reproach, on the other. Larra, moreover, wrote an essay, "Los Calaveras" (1835), in which he identified the nineteenth-century dandy as "el *calavera de buen tono* ... el emblema del siglo" (513; Larra's italics). Gustavo Adolfo Bécquer was also drawn to dandyism (Sebold 16–17; Moreno Hernández 48–50). Although Bécquer's personal style of dressing hardly qualified him as a dandy, his role as an arbiter of elegance (which he often assumed in his articles on fashion) did (Celaya 79–80).

Galdós's creation of Manuel Pez's dandylike appearance has not received much attention from critics. Even though as early as 1961, George J. Edberg called attention to the importance of Pez's manner of dress, he did not link don Manuel's elegance to dandyism. Similarly, in recent years, critics did not associate the fashionable politician with the figure of the dandy.[3] Instead, Pez's "dazzlingly impressive exterior" has been interpreted mostly as a sign of the protagonist's inner emptiness and vanity (Smith 84; Tsuchiya, "The Construction" 41) and as an effective tool for his sexual conquest of Rosalía (Tubert 385; Bly, *Pérez Galdós* 80). While Pez's elaborate attire and emphasis on his *toilette* can certainly be viewed as an emblem of his egotism, ostentation, and snobbishness, the abundance of sartorial details used in his portrait points to a great deal more than merely the negative side of his character.

Before entering the world of Galdós's protagonist, it is worth mentioning that prior to the nineteenth century the image of a man of fashion had been presented in the writings of Spanish moralists and social commentators mainly in a negative light. In the sixteenth century, Fray Tomás de Trugillo complained in his *Libro llamado reprobación de trajes, y abuso de juramentos* (1563) that the increasing multifariousness in men's wardrobes made it harder to determine one's standing in society and insisted that every man should not dress according to the dictates of fashion but "según la cualidad de su persona, estado y oficio" (qtd. in Vigil 195). A century later, Bartolomé Ximénez Patón dedicated an extensive passage in his *Discurso de los tufos, copetes y calvas* (1639) to ridiculing men who spent most of their time "en hacerse la barba, torcerse el bigote, levantar el copete, y peinar las guedexas, ampollar los cogotes, que la más hermosa dama" (qtd. in Vigil 196).[4] Similarly, in the eighteenth century, Juan Antonio Zamácola described fashionable men unfavorably. In addition to calling them "chuchumecos, raquíticos, contrahechos y afiligranados, que parecen manequines o muñecos modelados por algún mal aprendiz" (7–8), he linked their presumed effeminacy to the corruption of morals and the degeneracy of the Spanish race.[5] While throughout the sixteenth, seventeenth, and eighteenth centuries most writers considered excessive care of the body and fondness for stylish wardrobes highly improper for a man, in the nineteenth century, the attitude toward fashion and men of fashion changed.[6] As ready-made clothing began to expand in the late 1820s and forty years later came to dominate the men's clothing market, more and more essayists and authors of conduct books were urging their male readers to dress according to the dictates of fashion.[7] "La moda es la más inconstante de las fingidas divinidades, pero es la que tiene más adoradores. Su imperio se estiende por do quiera, y hay cierta especie de sabiduría en no ir contra ella" (86), Mariano de Rementería y Fica advised his readers as early as 1830 in his translation of the manual *El hombre fino al gusto del día: Manual completo de urbanidad, cortesía y buen tono*.[8] However, as one can see in Ramón de Mesonero Romanos's portrait of middle-class Spaniards wearing an allegedly unchanging, sober uniform in his social sketch *El Gabán* (1840), the recommendations to dress *à la mode* had hardly any effect on men (134). According to Mesonero Romanos, as the century advanced, men seemed to renounce progressively their claims to personal enhancement and beautification leaving the matter of dressing chic to women. However, Antonio Flores's detailed account of the variety of outfits of a *pollo-dandy* in his essay "Los pollos de 1850" suggests otherwise. Similarly to Ramón de Navarrete, who through his portrayal of an overdressed male in his sketch "El elegante" (1843) showed that not all men refrained from sartorial pleasures and that some of them relished the reputation of "*Dandy, fashionable ... o ... lion*" (158; Navarette's italics), Flores offered sufficient evidence that nineteenth-century Spanish men were quite invested in fashion.[9]

Interestingly, the nineteenth-century Spanish man of fashion never evolved into a full-fledged dandy. At the time Antonio Flores and Ramón de Navarrete used the term *dandy* in their respective essays, the word itself (despite being applied decades earlier by Mariano de Rementería y Fica in *El hombre fino al gusto del día: Manual completo de urbanidad, cortesía y buen tono*) was still considered a neologism in Spain. According to Corominas, the word *dandy* was first defined in the *Diccionario de galicismos* (1855) by Rafael María Baralt, who described it as follows:

What Is a Man of Fashion?

"[D]onde quiera que aparezca este vocablo anglo-francés, póngase una nota que explique a la generalidad del pueblo español como el tal significa LINDO, LECHUGUINO, PISAVERDE" (202–03). Indeed, in Spain, throughout the nineteenth century the public used the term *dandy* as a non-discriminatory synonym for a fashionable man. Even later during the end of the nineteenth century, when readers were acquainted with writings such as Barbey d'Aurevilly's *Du dandyisme et de George Brummell* (1845), the dandy generally was confused with the snob (Celma Valero 126–30; Badenes 50–53).[10]

In nineteenth-century Spanish literature, the figure of the dandy was never represented as a type of his own. Although, as I have mentioned earlier, nineteenth-century Spanish authors experimented with dandyism, they did not create a character of the dandy per se. Instead, as Gloria Ortiz indicated, the dandy marks his presence in the Spanish narrative as the most "immediate and influential predecessor" of the *señorito* (13). Yet the dandy, in addition to his influence on the figure of the *señorito*, had quite an effect on the character that paradoxically considered himself immune to his charm: the bourgeois gentleman. A superficial look at both the dandy and the gentleman might lead to the conclusion that the two types of men had hardly anything in common. After all, the dandy with his self-proclaimed superiority, his credo of idleness and irresponsibility, was an affront to the middle-class man with his virtues of responsibility, energy, and equality. Yet, the bourgeois gentleman adopted far more from the dandy than he ever cared to admit. Even though the bourgeois male was quick to voice his disapproval of the dandy, the ease with which the fashionable *beau* navigated his way to the top of the social ladder, his talent for self-promotion, and the use he made of his clothes, poses, and wit, were not entirely lost on the middle-class man.[11] All in all, the dandy succeeded in becoming what the respectable middle-class man aspired to turn into: a new kind of aristocrat, an individual who, like Beau Brummell, could justify his ascendance in society by qualities other than aristocratic origin and wealth (Gagnier 51–99).

That the nineteenth-century bourgeois male emulated the dandy, while concurrently preserving the image of the proper gentleman, is illustrated well in Galdós's social sketch "El elegante"

(1893). Looking back at the sartorial presentation of nineteenth-century middle-class Spaniards, the author draws the reader's attention to the ultra-conservative, non-expressive codes of their attire:

> Somos, por el traje, los mayores mamarrachos que han visto las edades desde la famosa hoja de higuera o de parra. ... Hemos proscrito el color, adoptando el negro o los antipáticos tonos de cenizas y los grises y asfaltos más feos que es posible imaginar ... Hemos desterrado las tonalidades vivas ... las joyas, las plumas; nuestros mozalbetes se forran del mismo paño negro y fúnebre que reviste la personalidad de clérigo o del magistrado. (233)

However, Galdós's essay uncovers more than his dissatisfaction with men's style of dressing. The praise of the simplicity, uniformity, and comfort of the monk's robe, which the writer contrasts with bourgeois men's apparel, brings to light his critique of middle-class men's exaggerated attention to the outward appearance and their feverish consumption of fashion. Of course, Galdós's description of bourgeois men's dandylike preoccupation with the external image was hardly novel at the time he wrote his essay. In what follows, we shall see that the author of *La de Bringas* already addressed the importance of clothes and the dandylike cult of self in his portrait of Manuel Pez.

At first sight, Manuel Pez's clothes appear to serve two purposes: to make him look like a respectable high-ranking official to the outside world and like an attractive lover to Rosalía Bringas. Dressed elegantly, but always in the same style and without divulging his effort to look chic, Pez is effective in preserving the image of an upright, middle-class gentleman:

> Mañana y tarde, Pez vestía de la misma manera, con levita cerrada de paño, pantalón que parecía estrenado el mismo día y chistera reluciente, sin que este esmero pareciese afectado ni revelara esfuerzo o molestia en él. ... Llevaba a todas partes el empaque de la oficina, y creeríase que levita, pantalón y sombrero eran parte integrante de la oficina misma, de la Dirección, de la Administración ... (108)

Later, the narrator describes Rosalía's impression of Pez's attire and demeanor as follows:

> Pez se agigantaba más cada día a sus ojos ... aquel aire elegante ... aquellos cuellos como el ampo de la nieve, altos, tiesos; aquel

What Is a Man of Fashion?

> pantalón que parecía estrenado el mismo día (170–71) ¡Oh, qué hombre tan extraordinario y fascinador! … ¡Y qué finura y distinción de modales …! (195)

Yet, things are rarely what they appear to be in Galdós's narrative. While his fashionable appearance seems to aid don Manuel in seducing Rosalía, ultimately, it is not his gentlemanly façade that makes Bringas's wife fall into his arms but his promise to protect her should she ever find herself in difficulties. Similarly, while the formal outfit seems to contribute greatly to his image as a serious bureaucrat, in reality the exaggerated neatness of his frock coat and the cleanliness of his body make it obvious that Pez's existence is devoted to the creation of his external image. There is no doubt that Galdós uses Pez's cultivation of his image throughout the novel to highlight the negative aspects of his personality. Like most of Galdós's fashion-oriented, male protagonists, the elegant politician fits easily in what Gabriel Cabrejas calls "una enciclopedia de hombres inútiles" whose modish look reflects on their self-centered, effeminate, and corrupt nature (157). However, the unappealing qualities of Pez deserve deeper scrutiny because they provide readers with an image that is far more complex than a simple picture of him as "a stereotypical product of a hypocritical society" (Tsuchiya, "The Construction" 41). The many references to Pez's pursuit of elegance and the author's portrayals of the stylish bureaucrat as a man dedicated solely to his own perfection link him not only to the social vices of the time but also to the figure of the dandy.

Like most of the dandylike characters penned by nineteenth-century Spanish novelists, such as Clarín's Álvaro Mesía, Galdós's Pez shares only some of the characteristics of the dandy. One of his most cited traits is his penchant for fashion and obsession with personal hygiene. "Vestía este caballero casi casi como un figurín," announces the narrator at the outset of the novel (107). In contrast to Francisco Bringas, who wears the "*levisac* de lanilla" made six years ago and "el sombrero de paja" that makes him look as if he "acababa de venir de La Habana," Pez dresses up for the summer in "el ligero y elegante traje de alpaca de color" (178; 243; 227).[12] For don Manuel, however, fashion does not necessarily mean merely wearing garments appropriate for the season. As Moers wrote, "the ideal of the dandy is cut in cloth" (21). Consequently, Pez's elegance, like the elegance of any dandy, has very little to do with excessive ornamentation or, to use Moers's words, "fantastic colours and frills, exotic jewels" (31). Rather, it has to do with a different style, one that, as Elizabeth Wilson put it, "was already coming into fashion, a style in which the most important element was fit" (*Adorned in Dreams* 180). "Su ropa tenía la virtud de no ajarse ni empolvarse nunca, y le caía sobre el cuerpo como pintada," says the narrator about Pez's impeccable appearance (107–08). Later, he emphasizes again the politician's affection for the superior cut and fit of his clothes by drawing Rosalía's attention to "aquella levita negra cerrada, sin una mota, planchada, estirada, cual si hubiera nacido en la misma piel del sujeto" (170–71).

Hygiene is the other trait that links Pez to the tradition of dandyism. The description of don Manuel's flawlessly shaved face, adorned by "patillas y bigote de oro oscuro ... limpios, relucientes, declarando en su brillo que se les consagraba un buen ratito en el tocador," emulates the archetype of all dandies, the great Beau Brummell (107). "Brummell's major contribution to history was his ... advocacy of cleanliness," wrote Moers (32). "His laborious toilette commenced with a furious scrubbing of the teeth ... Then he would shave with extreme care ... wash and scrub and wash again with plenty of good soap and hot water ..." (Moers 32–33). The narrator further underscores Pez's dandylike attitude toward his *toilette* by indicating how little cleanliness means to other men in the novel. Compared to Francisco Bringas, who saves on using soap and, according to his own wife's complaints, "se opone a que el aguador ... suba dos cubas más de agua, porque, según él, con mojarse el palmito ya basta," Pez with "aquel discreto uso de finos perfumes" and with "aquellas manos de mujer cuidadas con esmero ..." presents himself as a real dandy (130; 172; 171). Finally, there is the carefully thought-out repertoire of poses and gestures that Pez adopts while charming Bringas's wife with his sartorial grace. The scene of Pez walking with Rosalía shows that don Manuel, like all dandies, is essentially a theatrical being:

> Pez y Rosalía ... salían a dar vueltas por la terraza. ... Él, con la mano izquierda en el bolsillo del pantalón, recogido el borde de la levita, accionaba levemente con la derecha, empuñando un junco por la mitad. (109)

Yet, Galdós's Pez is different from the classic nineteenth-century dandy. Unlike the traditional dandy, who proudly assumed the

What Is a Man of Fashion?

role of the pioneer in the art of dressing, don Manuel follows the current fashion trend, instead of setting it. Further, Galdós's protagonist lacks what the nineteenth-century dandy was most famous for (in addition to his unique style of dressing): his rebellious nature (Moers 26–28). "Rebelliousness is at the heart of dandyism" asserted José Ignacio Badenes in his study on the dandy (12). "The dandy expresses his rebelliousness against the status quo by affirming the self through individuality and originality" (Badenes 13). "He works actively," wrote Badenes, "to create himself as a work of art, defying in his own person the standards which bourgeois society has codified at all levels for everyone to conform" (13).

That don Manuel, in contrast to the traditional dandy, conforms to the established order of bourgeois society and, what is more, greatly benefits from its structure, is evident from Galdós's descriptions of the bureaucrat's corrupt nature. What is perhaps not so obvious is that the author made further effort to highlight the lack of originality and individuality in Pez by depicting him as a mass-produced commodity: a dressmaker's dummy. "[S]u cara simpática, sin arrugas, [parecía] admirablemente conservada" (107). "[S]u áureo bigote … por la igualdad de los pelos, parecía artificial" (186). His body, despite the passing years, does not show any sign of aging. For, as the narrator tells us, although don Manuel is fifty, he looks a lot closer to forty. "Eran cincuenta años que parecían poco más de cuarenta" (107).

The novelist further intensifies Pez's mannequin-like appearance by superseding his living body with material objects. The only parts of Pez's flesh ever mentioned in the novel are his ever-friendly face and his clean, sterile hands. The sartorial goods out of which the modish bureaucrat creates himself seem to replace the rest. Moreover, as observed by Julian Palley, "nunca entramos completamente en la mente de don Manuel ni estamos seguros de sus móviles" (156). By replacing don Manuel's thoughts and feelings with a sum of artificial, premeditated gestures and poses, Galdós presents Pez as a man "incapaz de entusiasmo por nada" (106). The politician's face, like the face of any dressmaker's dummy, never reveals anything except "un reposo semejante … al de los santos que gozan la bienaventuranza eterna" (107). In addition, the association between cheap, mechanically reproduced cards and the image of Manuel Pez captured in Rosalía's thoughts reveals the difference between Galdós's protagonist and the dandy.

Chapter Two

> Pez, cada vez más frío, con un cierto airecillo de persona superior a las miserias humanas, continuaba hablando de cosas indiferentes con admirable seso. ... Su parecido con el Santo Patriarca antojósele a Rosalía más vivo que nunca; pero consideró aquella belleza rubia como la más sosa perfección del mundo. No le faltaba más que la vara de azucenas para pasar a figurar en la cartulina de los cromos de a peseta que se venden por las calles. (266)

Unlike the conventional dandy, Galdós's character is not a man who aspires to turn his persona into a unique and irreplaceable object of art, but a man who delights in his manufactured artifice and takes pleasure in making, to use Garelick's words, "an art form of commodifying personality" (3). Finally, there is the contrast between the classic dandy, who openly professed his love for finery and the lifestyle of a *bon vivant*, and Pez, who, despite his fondness for luxury and leisure, insists on preserving the image of himself as a serious politician and a commendable employee of the Spanish Civil Service. "Era este Pez el hombre más correcto que se podía ver, modelo excelente del empleado que llaman *alto* ... hombre que en su persona y estilo llevaba como simbolizadas la soberanía del Gobierno y ... de la Administración" (106; Galdós's italics).

The description of Manuel Pez as a man who resembles and, at the same time, differs from the typical dandy, presents an unflattering portrait of the nineteenth-century, bourgeois man in Spain. However, by placing the emphasis on Pez's dandylike elegance and his involvement in the excessive consumption of fashion, Galdós not only challenged the prevalent image of the bourgeois man as an embodiment of sartorial sobriety and uniformity, but also cast doubt on the protagonist's adherence to models of conventional masculinity. Although throughout the nineteenth century authors of etiquette manuals encouraged men to take care of their outward appearance, they underlined moderation, and not excess, as essential to achieving true elegance. In *La elegancia en el trato social: Reglas de etiqueta y cortesanía en todos los actos de la vida* (1898), Viscountess Bestard de la Torre made the following comment with respect to the male *toilette:*

> Un hombre que pretende el título de elegante ... no se viste desde por la mañana como un diplomático en día de recepción, pues sabe perfectamente que el traje negro de levita o frac ... son inadmisibles hasta la hora de las visitas. ... El verdadero

What Is a Man of Fashion?

> hombre culto, sin darse cuenta, llega a ser un modelo de elegancia y de buen tono, porque se inicia instintivamente en todos los usos, *sin darles importancia excesiva*. (40–43; my italics)

Thus, even though Pez makes an effort to hide his exaggerated attention to his *toilette*, the perfectly fitting clothing, the expensive accessories and perfumes that the narrator brings to surface in the dandylike portrayals of him, attest to a lack of moderation and self-control in the art of dressing. Additionally, they draw attention to a weakness commonly associated with women, namely, excessive consumerism. Of course, as a consumer of sartorial goods, Manuel Pez differs from Rosalía Bringas and from other male characters in Galdós's narrative who overspend on finery. Nineteenth-century men, as the American fashion historian Anne Hollander explained, "didn't brood at home over fashion plates" (*Sex and Suits* 118). Unlike their wives and daughters, men did not "go to several different fabric stores and study many varieties of texture and fiber, and shop around for different colors for facings, and compare the thicknesses of ornamental braid or the sizes of buttons …" (Hollander, *Sex and Suits* 118). The fashionable look was something that nineteenth-century, middle-class men procured directly from their tailors. Consider, for example, Milagros's complaint about her husband spending lavishly on his tailor: "¡Ay!, créalo usted, mi mariducho tiene la culpa de que vivamos de esta manera … He tenido que pagarle ayer una cuenta de su sastre, que se había colgado de la campanilla de la puerta de casa …" (135–36).[13] Although Galdós is not as explicit about Pez's consumerism (the novelist does not describe the politician's visits to a tailor nor to any other luxury establishments) as he was about the shopping habits of Agustín Caballero in *Tormento* (1884) and, later on, of José María Bueno de Guzmán in *Lo prohibido* (1885), the emphasis on the details of don Manuel's elaborate appearance are clear indicators of his acquisitive appetite. Significant in this context is also Pez's lax attitude toward female consumerism. Unable to restrain himself from indulging in sartorial excess, the fancy bureaucrat proves to be equally incapable of imposing the virtue of self-control and moderation on others. "Sus hijas le mareaban con las frecuentes excursiones a Bayona para comprar trapos … se traían a España media Francia" (231), the narrator tells us about his daughters' uncontrolled consumption of fashion. Moreover, in his letter to Rosalía, Pez confirms his lenience toward

Chapter Two

his daughters' obsession with material pleasures: "*Este viaje me ha arruinado ... A las niñas se les antojaba todo lo que veían en Bayona ... He gastado la renta de un año ...*" (270; Galdós's italics).

The exaggerated attention to dress and fashion and excessive consumerism are not the only aspects of Pez that allow the narrator to question the image of a bourgeois male and to cast doubt on the protagonist's compliance with dictates of normative masculinity. The dandylike depiction of this character (in particular with reference to his overstated elegance) is significant in that it helps the writer ridicule what the nineteenth-century, middle-class men's outward appearance was supposed to stand for: the bourgeois values of thrift, merit, and work. The exquisite accessories, such as "aquella olorosa cartera de cuero de Rusia," that make Manuel Pez look so noble and gentlemanly in Rosalía's eyes, do not attest to the bureaucrat's thrift (172). It also is obvious that Galdós does not place the traditional uniform of bourgeois men (the frock coat, trousers, and top hat) on don Manuel's body to accentuate his work ethic but rather his lack thereof. After all, the narrator never describes Pez working inside his office. "En fin, don Manuel había tomado en aborrecimiento su domicilio, y estaba en él lo menos posible. La tranquilidad no existía para él más que en la oficina, donde no hacía más que fumar y recibir a los amigos ..." (112). Thus, if "energy was one of the most frequent and most characteristic terms associated with male activity in this period" (Barker-Benfield 338), the exaggerated neatness of Pez's appearance only exacerbates the contrast between his idleness and apathy and the bourgeois model of an active and industrious masculinity. "Considerábase superior a sus contemporáneos, al menos veía más, columbraba otra cosa mejor, y como no lograba llevarla a la realidad, de aquí su flemática calma" (187).

Additionally, there are the allusions to Pez's non-normative manhood in his self-conscious aestheticization. Although, unlike the prototypical dandy who strives to transform himself into a unique object of art, the politician turns his body into a mass-produced commodity, the narrator exploits his appearance of a dressmaker's dummy to highlight not only his constructedness and the denial of his authentic interiority, but also his nonconformity to the dominant norms of sexual behavior. Given that it is Rosalía who "acts as the aggressor in her relationship with Pez" (McKinney 91) and in doing so deviates from the feminine pattern of sexual passivity, it is evident that the couple reversed the conventional sexual roles. Although Pez ultimately escapes the role of the prey, he too diverges from the paradigm of sexual conduct prescribed for his gender in that he accepts (as we can deduce from the narrator's providing mainly Rosalía's impressions of the bureaucrat's sartorial appeal and not the other way around) the feminine position of an object of gaze. Additionally, one could argue that the narrator used Pez's self-aestheticization and Rosalía's perspective on it to hint at the protagonist's lack of natural sexuality. As mentioned earlier, the dressmaker's dummy appearance of don Manuel reinforces the image of him as a man who is devoid of passion and physicality (except for brief mentions of his feminine hands and face). However, ultimately, it is Rosalía's dealings with Pez and her response to his mannequin-like appearance that shed light on his questionable sexuality. While the lady is certainly attracted to the politician's impeccable elegance, it is not his manly beauty that she associates with his stylish image (references to Pez's erotic/masculine charm are, in fact, conspicuously absent from her daydreaming about him) but the material value that his outfits display and the promise of financial reward that prompt the adultery. Ironically, despite the differences between the unassuming Francisco Bringas and the fashionable politician, both men are incapable of inciting sexual interest in Rosalía. In one way or the other, whether in the narrator's direct depiction of Pez or in his transcriptions of Rosalía's thoughts of him or her husband ("Aquel muñeco hízola madre de cuatro hijos" [196]) both men's lack of natural sexuality is implied through allusions to them as male dolls.

Considering the use that Galdós's contemporaries made of the dandy/aesthete figure in their respective retorts to the late-nineteenth-century crisis of gender, and masculinity in particular (Tsuchiya, *Marginal Subjects* 112–35), it is tempting to assume that the author created his portrait of the dandylike Pez to primarily mark the symptoms of this crisis already a decade earlier. Yet, if read in a different context, such as Weber's theory of the origin of modern capitalism, the image of Pez also reveals that Galdós linked his fashion-oriented, dandylike character to Spain's problematic insertion into modernity.

In his explanation of the reasons for which the West provided the most favorable conditions for the birth and dissemination of the spirit of modern capitalism, Weber pointed to the Protestant religion and the attitudinal factors that originated from the Protestant work ethic, such as frugality, rigorous organization of labor, and one's initiative in the systematic pursuit of profit. To prove that religious beliefs contributed in equal measure to the formation of modern capitalism along with industrial progress and technological innovations, the German scholar centered his interest in examining the differences between the Catholic and Protestant cultures. While Catholics strove for salvation through regular prayers, confession of sins, and good work, Protestants believed in achieving the same through methodical work and pursuit of wealth for God's glory. In consequence, two dissimilar attitudes toward economic activities and toward life in general developed between these two groups. While Protestantism rewarded one's pursuit of wealth, methodical work, and frugality through the promise of salvation and social prestige, Catholicism linked redemption to one's spiritual qualities.

Weber's observations are helpful for understanding the use that Galdós made of the dandylike and the non-dandylike features of Pez to shed light on Spain's uneven insertion into modernity. In drawing attention to the politician's dandylike love for fashion and idleness as well as his non-dandylike lack of originality and initiative, Galdós did not just create a character that embodied the opposite of the ideals that nourished the growth of modern capitalism in the West. By emphasizing the above characteristics in Pez, the novelist demonstrated that deficiency in cultural values (e.g., frugality, hard work, and individualism) was as much the cause of Spain's problematic transition to modernity as the insufficient economic growth and political stagnation.

Hardly accidental in this context is also the protagonist's marriage to Carolina, who propagates (whether sincerely or not) the Catholic belief in "*salvation through sacraments*" (129; Weber's italics), and the bureaucrat's participation in the Maundy Thursday ceremony, which exemplifies (despite being a farce) the concept of redemption "through good works" (Weber 128). Through his description of Pez, who turns Sunday services into a time of idle talk with friends or uses the Maundy Thursday ceremony as an opportunity to display (like the ladies around him) his fine clothes, the narrator surely made clear that "religion appears only in a hollow external form" among the Spanish bourgeoisie (Bly, *Pérez Galdós* 60). Nevertheless, the politician's behavior also enabled the narrative voice to show that the Catholic Church did not stimulate the spirit of change, let alone the spirit of modern capitalism. Instead of encouraging frugality, low-key simplicity, or one's engagement in productive activities, the Church endorsed the opposite: pomp, glitter, apathy, and the preservation of social and political status quo.

Yet, where the fashionable image of Pez allowed Galdós to point out Spain's problematic transition to modernity in a most explicit manner, the references to him show him as a man who is different from a true dandy. By endowing the politician with characteristics that differentiate him from the traditional dandy, that is, by portraying him as a follower of fashion and a dressmaker's dummy, the novelist not only voiced his critique of Spanish bourgeois men's dependence on foreign ideals of masculinity (at least in the matter of dressing) and, consequently, a failure to create their own cultural identity. Through the image of a passive, mannequin-like Pez, Galdós also exposed the lack of vitality and initiative of Spanish middle-class men who failed to move away from the prevalent values and *structures* of the Ancien Regime. While the nineteenth-century conventional dandy was, as Baudelaire described him, an individual "full of fire, passion, courage and … native energy" (28), willing to break away from the shackles of the past, Galdós's mannequin-like Pez is a man who epitomizes a different spirit. He embodies the image of "esa España dormida, beatífica, que se goza en ser juguete de los sucesos y en nada se mete con tal que la dejen comer tranquila" (Pérez Galdós, *La de Bringas* 107). Furthermore, to reinforce the idea that his character (and, by extension, Spanish bourgeois men in general) preferred to abstain from taking the risk to engage in a productive activity that would lead to Spain's true modernization, Galdós's narrator brings forward not only Pez's own apathy and sleepiness. He also draws attention to the contagious effect that Pez's dressmaker's dummy appearance, idle talk, and lack of energy impart on others. "Por mi parte, confieso que el modo de hablar de aquel señor tan guapín … ejercía no sé qué acción narcótica sobre mis nervios … ya me parecía que un dulce beleño se derramaba en mi cerebro, y el sillón de doña Tula … me convidaba a dormir" (185–86).

In conclusion, the would-be dandy portrait of Pez shows that Galdós did not reduce the depiction of his protagonist's love for fashion merely to expose his moral shortcomings. Instead, through the portrayal of Pez as a man who resembles and, simultaneously, differs from the traditional dandy, Galdós cast doubt on his adherence to the paradigms of his gender and denounced some of the reasons for Spain's uneven entry into modernity. Dandyism, as Baudelaire explained in "The Painter of Modern Life," "appears above all in periods of transition, when democracy is not yet all-powerful, and aristocracy is only just beginning to totter and fall" (28). Hence, it is not surprising that Galdós turned to the figure of the dandy while creating the character of Pez in his brilliant re-enactment of the 1868 Revolution in *La de Bringas*. Nevertheless, Galdós's Pez is not a full-fledged dandy. This partial resemblance is not accidental either, considering the author's disappointment with the short-lived results of the September uprising and his discontent with the Spanish bourgeoisie's lack of vitality and initiative to move away from the prevalent values and structures of the Ancien Regime. With the image of Pez as a partial dandy and the depiction of him as an individual whose compliance with the dictates of normative masculinity remains questionable, Galdós made unambiguous his criticism of bourgeois men's inability to take a full lead in the political system of the post-1868 Spain and, thus, his disillusionment with incompleteness of Spanish modernization. Up to date only in his exterior, the would-be dandy Pez personifies the desire of nineteenth-century Spanish middle-class men (and the Spanish bourgeoisie in general) to look and feel modern without undergoing any substantial changes in their ways of living (Valis, *The Culture* 11). Trendy on the exterior, but unmanly and inert at the core, the fashionable politician incarnates the illusion of progress and aptly captures the novelist's critical view of the bourgeois Spaniards' superficial idea of modernity.

Of course, Galdós was not the only writer who considered the art of dressing an appropriate vehicle for examining the increasingly problematic notions of gender and for noting the need to redefine the traditional limits of femininity and masculinity as a vital step in Spain's project of modernization. As we shall see in the following chapters, fashion with its potential to uphold and to challenge the conventional gender order, furnished Pardo Bazán with an effective medium to question the prevailing notions of bourgeois womanhood and manhood. In comparison to Galdós, however, doña Emilia took it a step further in her deployment of fashion. As we will see in her portrayals of female and male protagonists in *Insolación*, through the skillful manipulation of sartorial features, Pardo Bazán not only brought to light contradictions and ambiguities in the normative notions of gender. She also ventured to explore via references to elegant outfits, accessories, and beauty products new models of femininity and masculinity in late-nineteenth-century Spain.

Chapter Three

Fashion and Femininity in Pardo Bazán's *Insolación*

Perhaps none of Pardo Bazán's female characters has irritated contemporary critics as much as Asís Taboada, the protagonist of *Insolación* (1889). Financially independent and free from patriarchal authority, the young marquesa scandalized commentators of her time with her promiscuous and supposedly unladylike behavior. Pereda, for example, complained about the lack of propriety in Asís's conduct in his February 1891 review in *El Imparcial*. He describes how she accepts an invitation from a man she barely knows to go to the San Isidro Fair and there "se mete con él en figones y merenderos, se emborracha, etc., etc." (*Las comezones* 1009). Pereda's colleague, Emilio Bobadilla (Fray Candil), portrayed Asís as "una tía, mal que pese a doña Emilia" (qtd. in Penas Varela 29–30). Clarín discredited the Galician widow by simply stating that she was a nobody.[1] Fortunately, in recent years, critical response to this novel and the protagonist has changed radically. Numerous studies dedicated to Pardo Bazán's symbolic and cultural representation of her protagonist's body demonstrate that scholars have discovered the complexity and richness of doña Emilia's character.[2] However, while the marquesa's body has received much critical attention in recent decades, surprisingly, no studies have been dedicated to the adornment of her body and the manner in which Asís's fashionable *toilettes* convey the author's views on changing ideals of femininity in late-nineteenth-century Spain.

Sartorial fashion was a subject of strong interest to Pardo Bazán (Ruíz-Ocaña 373–78; Sinovas Maté 149–55; 509–13). The sheer number of doña Emilia's essays on women's clothing and accessories shows that the writer was a keen observer of the latest innovations in feminine apparel. Moreover, many of her comments from the 1880s and 1890s on the appearance of shorter skirts and bloomers in Spain indicate that for Pardo Bazán the new

Chapter Three

trends in the womanly art of dressing were promising signs of a coming change in women's mentalities and life conditions (Zárate 175–78).

During the final decades of the nineteenth century—whether in Spain or in the rest of Europe (see Silverman)—neither the new fashion for women nor the feminist movement was viewed in a positive light. The image of a modern woman wearing a divided skirt, smoking a cigarette, or riding a bicycle was perceived as a menace to the traditional ideals of femininity and, as such, was largely ridiculed in Spanish periodicals (Tolliver, *Cigar Smoke* 43–65; López Fernández 294–97). However, the modern *femme* was not the one-dimensional cultural phenomenon that late-nineteenth-century publications and drawings attempted to portray. Depicted by some as an individual who uses neither "velo ni sombrero, anda 'con paso elástico de mujer no estorbada ni por corsé si por tacones' y emana un atractivo sin artificios" (Bordonada 101) and by others as a richly adorned sensual being (Litvak 161–72), the modern woman was a complex cultural construct. She was, as Pardo Bazán demonstrated in *Insolación*, a figure whose daring posture and sartorial splendor marked her as an individual torn by opposing desires: "the desire to attract, and the desire to rise superior to that desire" (Cunnington, *Feminine Attitudes* 290). In what follows, I examine the role of feminine *toilettes* in Pardo Bazán's construction of the modern woman. More specifically, I explore the ways in which fashion in *Insolación* is implicated in the reinforcement and subversion of the established gender order and in which beauty products, clothing, and accessories function to signal the ambivalent nature of late-nineteenth-century femininity in Spain.

Before entering Pardo Bazán's novelistic boudoir and discussing the representations of her protagonist's sartorial beauty in detail, it is worth mentioning that women's use of beauty products had been associated with moral infirmity prior to the nineteenth century. In the sixteenth century, in *La perfecta casada* (1583), Fray Luis de León connected female beauty aids to deception, ugliness, and dirt and composed long passages to convince his readers that a woman's desire to wear makeup was proportional to "amor proprio desordenadísimo, apetito insaciable de vana excelencia … deshonestidad arraygada en el corazón" (150). Although cosmetics might improve a female's appearance, admitted Juan de Zabaleta a century later in his collection of social sketches, *El día de fiesta por la mañana y por la tarde* (1654), "una mujer ... más blanca que la nieve, las cejas como de ébano, las mejillas como de rosa, los labios como de coral y la garganta como de alabastro" (114–15) is a dishonest person and therefore not a desirable candidate for a wife. Similarly, in the eighteenth century Gabriel Quijano in *Vicios de las tertulias y concurrencias del tiempo* ... (1785) associated the use of beauty aids with female idleness, vanity, and corruption of morals in general (179–81). However, the nineteenth century marked a change in the fairer sex's attitude toward fashion and the application of beauty products in Spain. As cosmetics, once regarded as luxuries available primarily to upper-class women, began to be produced and distributed on a larger scale, more and more perfumeries were established in Madrid offering all kinds of exquisite beauty aids to female clientele. According to Ángel Fernández de los Ríos, as early as 1835, "llamaron la atención general la perfumería de Diana ... en la calle del Caballero de Gracia, y una tienda de quincalla" (654). There, women could chose from such exclusive products as "las perlas de Paraguay para las canas, las cremas de pepinos o de caracol para el cutis o el agua de Ninon de Lenclos" (qtd. in Gonzalo Menéndez Pidal 190).

The rich assortment of new beauty aids alone, of course, did not cause the change in attitude toward makeup. However, with the array of new cosmetics available to middle-class (and even working-class) women in the second half of the century, the conservative commentators' calls for abstinence from beauty aids seem to have fallen on deaf ears.[3] As the cosmetics industry continued to grow and develop into an important sector of the women's market in the last decades of the nineteenth century, the use of makeup and perfume became not only socially accepted but even encouraged for female customers in Spain. "¡Que se pinta! Sí señor. ... ¿Y qué ha de hacer?," wrote Manuel Matoses in his 1872 social sketch, *Las que se pintan*, in which he openly defended a woman's right to self-embellishment (222). Yet, the proliferation of beauty aids did more than simply provide women with the opportunity to improve on nature. In addition to stimulating creativity, cosmetics, alongside dresses and accessories, became an effective visual means of women's self-expression and a central element in the construction of female identity.[4]

The idea of sartorial art as a medium in the construction and representation of the feminine self was also a recurrent subject of Pardo Bazán's writings. For instance, her articles on fashion

Chapter Three

during her years as a reporter of the World Exhibition in Paris in 1889 and again in 1890 are more than mere descriptions of the latest designs. In addition to providing examples from the past and present of how changes in women's dressing styles contribute to shaping new ideals of feminine beauty, the novelist used the complexity and contradictions of fashion to problematize, in Catharina Vallejo's words, "the limits of female gender ... in both transgressing and confirming them" (455). The amazement in doña Emilia's tone in her description of luxurious accessories, for example, conforms to the traditional attitude of women toward fashion. "Hoy se emplea la joyería en menudencias de tocador ... Los cepillos, peines, limpia-uñas ... y los ... anteojos de tallo largo, más de moda que nunca, llevan sobre la rubia concha cifra de diamantes" (*Al pie de la Torre Eiffel* 227). Likewise, Pardo Bazán's account of modish items such as shoes and stockings, which she depicts on a passive female body ("las señoras elegantes que se dejan pasear en sillón de ruedas a través de la Exposición" [*Al pie de la Torre Eiffel* 224]) ably reinforces the customary image of a nineteenth-century elegant woman of leisure. At the same time, Pardo Bazán's articles in favor of wearing divided skirts call attention to a more active and independent type of femininity. Even though the author was aware that the divided skirt would mostly benefit working-class women, since it would make it easier for them to travel to work, "recorrer las calles aunque llueva o haga frío ... bajar y subir cuestas" (*La reforma racional del traje* 3), she considered it also advantageous to ladies of her own class. By describing how the split skirt would improve life for bourgeois and upper-class women in terms of "el movimiento, la gimnasia de los músculos, el largo paseo ..." (*La reforma racional del traje* 3), the novelist encouraged the fairer sex to move away from the impractical way of dressing. Moreover, doña Emilia urged the conventional woman of leisure to renounce the unhealthy lifestyle, which she depicted as "una vida sedentaria y enervante que la pone anémica y ahilada a modo de planta cuanta vegeta en sitio oscuro" (*La reforma racional del traje* 3). Pardo Bazán's promotion of the divided skirt did not mean that she wanted women to imitate men's style of dress. "Del traje masculino les aconsejaría huir como del fuego" (*Más indumentaria* 1), wrote the novelist in December of 1889 in *El Imparcial*. Depicted as an essentially feminine garment ("el *divided skirt* no es sino una falda ..." [*La reforma racional del traje*

3]), which, nevertheless, enabled women to move freely outside the domestic sphere (an activity more proper for a nineteenth-century male than female), the divided skirt draws attention, under Pardo Bazán's pen, not to the reversal but rather to the shifting nature of traditional gender divides.

Inseparable from her views on gender issues, the author's observations of the female art of dressing not only bring into focus the role fashion played in shaping new images of femininity in Spain but also are illustrative of the way Pardo Bazán wrestled with her portrait of the modern woman. The different images of a modish *femme* that emerge in doña Emilia's essays on fashion indicate that in the late nineteenth century, definitions of femininity had been fragmented and that it was no longer possible to write of them as a single unified concept. Just as fashion's growing complexity had made it more difficult to keep abreast of the array of fabrics, colors, and styles, it was equally challenging to mark out the unstable boundaries of modern womanhood. Hence, it is in fashion and its connection to the modern urban world, its rapidly changing range of styles, and its potential to accommodate and to challenge the conventional limits of gender that Pardo Bazán found a fitting medium to convey the multiple and controversial images of the contemporary woman. As we shall see in *Insolación*, the novelist frequently resorted to the rich assortment of feminine *toilettes* to articulate the manner in which Asís Taboada upholds and at the same time subverts the traditional gender order and to draw attention to the ambivalent, changing nature of late-nineteenth-century femininity in Spain.

In *Insolación*, Asís Taboada is described as a well-groomed elegant woman, who enjoys dressing stylishly but, unlike other Pardo Bazán characters (Ezama Gil 2005), is not consumed by her fascination with fashion: "Entretenía sus ocios pensando … que el último vestido que le había mandado su modista era tan gracioso y menos caro que el de Worth de la Sahagún …" (163–64). In fact, a quick look at the author's descriptions of Asís's cleanliness, the plainness of her hairstyle, and her unpretentious way of dressing might lead one to conclude that the novelist used cosmetics and articles of clothing to emphasize that the protagonist is a truly elegant woman whose charm lies in sartorial simplicity. So Asís is portrayed as a lady who wears "un traje serio, de señora que aspira a no llamar la atención" (168) and "el peinado sobrio, sin postizos ni rellenos" (221). In contrast to the working-class women at the San Isidro Fair, "una chula de mantón terciado, peina de bolas, brazos desnudos" (129) and "una gitanuela ... el pelo azulado de puro negro ... recogido en castaña, con su peina de cuerno y su clavel sangre de toro" (134), the main character distinguishes herself by her attire that is simple, elegant, and appropriate for the occasion. Asís's choice of colors for her outfit and hat, "el sombrero negro de paja con cinta escocesa" (98), also stresses the protagonist's good taste. "Varios motivos se reunían para completar mi satisfacción" (105), Asís tells the reader while recalling her trip to the fair. "Mi traje de *céfiro* gris sembrado de anclitas rojas, era de buen gusto en una excursión matinal como aquella; mi sombrero negro de paja me sentaba bien, según comprobé en el vidrio delantero de la berlina ..." (105). Overall, the protagonist's sartorial presentation echoes the author's observations on fashion in *Al pie de la Torre Eiffel*. In addition to describing Asís as modest yet sophisticated in her gray outfit, the novelist depicted her character wearing a hat that was light and unpretentious in its decoration and that resembled the style of women's hats, on which doña Emilia commented at length during her visit to the Universal Exposition in Paris in 1889. "Los sombreros de este año demuestran que la moda está en un buen momento de poesía unida a la razón. ... Así son los de ahora. Un casquetito que encaja perfectamente sobre el breve peinado actual; ... pocos cintajos, pocas plumas, ninguna bisutería ... Con la paja calada ... no pesan ni media libra" (*Al pie de la Torre Eiffel* 218–19).

However, Asís's appearance reveals more than good taste. In recent years, much has been written on ambivalence as one of the vital characteristics in the presentation of uncertainty and doubt in *Insolación* (Tolliver, "Narrative" 103–18; Valis, "Confession" 238–43; Karageorgou-Bastea 237–44).[5] According to Joyce Tolliver, ambivalence between the protagonist's "desire for conformity and a consciousness of her own transgression, and, on the other hand, a rejection of the implacability of the laws which she has transgressed" ("Narrative" 106) is essential to the dynamics of narrative perspective of this text. The recurrent alternation between narrative voices (and perspectives) of the protagonist and the narrator results in presenting the reader with "two simultaneous, mutually contradictory 'messages' ... one which ultimately upholds the sexual status quo of nineteenth-century bourgeois Spain and one which attacks it" (Tolliver, "Narrative" 104). It is through the manipulation of narrative perspective, wrote Tolliver, that "Pardo Bazán ... manages to affirm feminine sexual desire, but protects herself from accountability for that message through the narrative 'hedge' of the superficial conventional message" ("Narrative" 104).

While changes in narrative voice and manipulations of narrative perspectives are indeed effective tools at work here, they are not the only means by which the author conveyed Asís's vacillation between her wish to obey societal norms and her defiance of them. As we shall see, the different choices of the protagonist's *toilettes* also are implicated in the presentation of her conflicting desires. Consider the image of Asís at the beginning of the novel, dressed conservatively on her way to church ("iba yo con mi eucologio y mi mantillita hecha una santa" [91]) followed only a few pages later by the description of her in the middle of hectic preparations to look appealing in her suitor's presence. "Tenía que tomar el abanico, dejar el devocionario, cambiar mantilla por sombrero. ... Arreglarme el pelo, darme velutina, buscar un pañolito fino, escoger unas botas nuevas ... ponerme guantes frescos ... echarme en el bolsillo un *sachet* de raso que huele a *iris*" (97). Similarly, while the serious attire worn during the visit with her aunts reflects the protagonist's attempt to conform to patriarchal order ("De hoy más vuelvo a mi inflexible línea de conducta" [168]), her taking pains to appear attractive for another date with Pacheco points to Asís's transgression of societal mores by revealing once more her acquiescence to her sexual desire. "[P]ara dar con unos guantes nuevos tuvo que desbaratar el baúl ... para sacar un sombrero, desclavó dos cajones ... al cepillarse los dientes, se rompe el frasco del elixir contra el mármol del lavabo" (243).

However, the contrast between the two images of the protagonist (i.e., the conventionally attired lady who seeks to comply with the society's rules and the fashionable *femme* who breaks these rules by failing to repress her sexual urges) provides us with only a basic idea of Asís's contradictory desires. Given that the beauty of *Insolación* resides, as Penas Varela wrote, "en el entresijo de perspectivas que provocan diferentes valoraciones" (42) and that this novel "juega constantemente con el lector, y le exige moverse con habilidad en una auténtica malla si no quiere llegar a conclusiones equivocadas" (42), it should come as no surprise that it is not as much the contrast between these two images as the conflicting

Chapter Three

perspectives *within* these images that imbue Asís's portrait with ambiguities. To illustrate my point, let me return for a moment to the first description of Asís's grooming activities shortly before leaving for her trip with Pacheco. (I refer to the paragraph starting with the sentence: "tenía que tomar el abanico ... escoger unas botas ..." [97]). What might seem like an insignificant passage presenting Asís's manner of planning how to adorn herself for her date is of great importance, since each of the items she lists is preceded by the infinitive form of the verb. The use of the impersonal form before all of the articles of clothing lessens Asís's responsibility for the action and diminishes her presence as a subject here. In anticipation of Pacheco's gaze, the main character employs the sartorial goods to construct an image of herself as a beautiful woman for her suitor to contemplate. She, therefore, upholds conventional expectations of her gender by assuming the role of an aesthetically pleasing object of desire for men. "Porque al fin ... Pacheco era para mí persona de cumplido; íbamos a pasar algunas horas juntos y *observándonos muy de cerca ... no me gustaría que algún rasgo de mi ropa o mi persona le produjese efecto desagradable*" (98; my italics). Yet, as the presence of the reciprocal pronoun *nos*, as well as the choice of the verb *observar*, indicates, Asís's position as an object is only part of the story here. "Representing the body" (88), states Peter Brooks in his studies concerning the body in modern narratives, "seems always to involve viewing the body. ... While the bodies viewed are both male and female" (88), asserts Brooks, drawing from the study of the feminist film critic Laura Mulvey, "vision is typically a male prerogative, and its object of fascination the woman's body ..." (88). However, such a division is not the case in *Insolación*. As the main character's words ("observándonos muy de cerca" [98]) indicate, not only does Asís defend her right to her own specular subjectivity (and, hereby subverts the societal expectations of her gender) but also, as I mentioned before, she concurrently upholds these expectations by positioning herself consciously in the role of a fine-looking (i.e., stylishly-dressed) woman for her suitor to contemplate.

Conventional and simultaneously subversive is also the aforementioned image of Asís on her early morning walk to church at the outset of chapter 3: "iba yo con mi eucologio y mantillita hecha una santa" (91). Dressed in a *mantilla*, an attire associated commonly with Spanish women's adherence to tradition, the protagonist draws on the symbolic value of her outfit to emphasize the seriousness of her bearing.[6] However, this earnest stance is not so earnest after all, considering the marquesa's use of the diminutive—*mantillita*—and, as Mary Lee Bretz observed, "her obvious enjoyment of the street scenes and the compliments proffered by lower-class, street-smart young men" (401). In fact, the contradiction between the protagonist's formal posture and her unbecoming actions (i.e., taking note of her working-class admirers' tight-fitting pants ["recuerdo ... dos o tres de esos chulos de pantalón estrecho" (91)] and savoring their tactless accolades ["Trabajo me costó contener la risa al entreoír estos disparates ..." (92)]), produces in Asís's first-person narrative not just an ambiguous but also an ironic effect.

Pervasive throughout the novel, irony has attracted a great deal of critical attention. However, while early scholars, such as Robert M. Scari, viewed irony as an "instrumento cognoscitivo cuya funcíon ... es formular y resolver problemas vitales" (87), more recently, Christina Karageorgou-Bastea considered it as a means by which the principal voice of the novel tends to "proveer su mundo con facetas múltiples que se dirigen, por un lado, en contra de la seguridad de intenciones ideológicas intrínsecas ...y, por otro, en contra de la univocidad de interpretación" (243). According to Karageorgou-Bastea, "es la ironía la que salva del autoritarismo, la que posibilita la movilidad de un punto de vista, aparentemente, fijo ... [y] disminuye la gravedad del 'pecado' sugerido" (241). Although Karageorgou-Bastea's observations apply mainly to the voice of the third-person narrator, they also are relevant to the way the ironic tone functions in Asís's first-person account, in particular in reference to clothing. Not only does irony (which, as we have seen, arises from the inconsistency between the marquesa's conservative look and informal conduct) put a question mark over the protagonist's reliability as a narrator. Because of the light tone that it reinforces in her narrative, the irony also makes it possible for her to oscillate—without being judged too harshly—between two different manners of carrying herself in her *mantilla*.

The common perception of the *mantilla* as an emblem of Spanish national character and tradition was well documented, as I mentioned before, among nineteenth-century Spanish social commentators. However, while this viewpoint was popular among conservative (mostly male) authors (Strbáková 1003–04), ladies

Chapter Three

(according to the fashion correspondent for *El Semanario Pintoresco Español*, writing under the name, Clementina) had a different opinion on this matter. Commenting on the popularity of the Spanish *mantilla* in France in 1837 and the Spanish women's way of wearing it, the female journalist reported:

> Este gracioso capricho lo hemos tomado de las españolas, aunque ellas pretenden que jamás las francesas saben sacar todo el partido de un auxiliar tan poderoso de las gracias y la ligereza: dicen que ignora toda extranjera el modo garboso y señoril de llevar la seductora mantilla, cuyos más insignificantes pliegues dejan traslucir *la tierna imaginación y ocultas miras* de quien en ella se esconde. (qtd. in Pena González, *Traje* 210; my italics)

There is no doubt judging by the particulars in Asís's account of her morning walk at the beginning of chapter 3 that she made use of her *mantilla* as illustrated in the above passage. As observed before, the details included in her mentioning of the street-smart admirers' clothing and later on her description of the niceties in Pacheco's outward appearance make evident that the conservatively dressed marquesa did not shy away from subjecting these men to her gaze. However, if Asís concurrently breaks and upholds the patriarchal codes of feminine decorum during her encounter with the lower-class admirers in that she enjoys herself as both the viewed and the viewer, then, during her meeting with Pacheco she does something else. As her eyes register the Andalusian's external qualities, she places herself *exclusively* in the role traditionally defined as masculine—the bearer of look. She, thus, turns the tables on the traditional gender roles, in which, as Mulvey contended, the "pleasure in looking has been split between active/male and passive/female" (19) between "woman as image, man as bearer of the look" (19). She does so, by drawing further attention to her suitor's static position ("*parado* al pie de corpulento plátano" [93; my italics]), relishing his good looks ("la favorable impresión que me causaron las prendas personales del andaluz" [93]) and his sartorial allure: "Pacheco, que vestía un elegante terno gris claro, me pareció galán de veras ..." (94). Consequently, she casts him as "a passive image of visual perfection" (Mulvey 23), an object of her gaze and desire.[7]

The inconsistency between how one would expect Asís to behave in her *mantilla* and how she actually conducts herself provides an example of how a seemingly straightforward image of her includes an array of contradictory meanings. Conservative and subversive, object and subject, a figure to emulate and to condemn by continuously moving between and among those categories, the protagonist presents herself as a complex character who, beneath the protective coverage of irony, scripts her own pattern of behavior instead of performing the typecast role assigned to her gender by society. Equally telling is the irony that originates from the incongruities between what Asís says and what she does in reference to Pacheco's clothing. "Yo no me pago solamente del exterior" (94), declares the marquesa immediately after identifying all the fashionable features (e.g., the style and color of her suitor's outfit), and after portraying him (not only in this scene but also in the preceding chapter) mostly by the details of his clothing. "Pacheco, que llevaba con soltura el frac, me pareció distinguido …" (83), recalls Asís as her first impression of the handsome Andalusian in the previous chapter. By disclaiming what she already affirmed (more than once in her account), the protagonist not only makes her denial of don Diego's external appeal unconvincing but also confirms even further her strong physical attraction to his sartorial and bodily charms.

Humor, asserts the British feminist scholar Jane Arthurs, in her study of corporal decorum and the importance that modern *civilized* societies attach to women's control of "bodily posture … movements and … the language used to refer to bodily activities" (137), is one of the few cultural arenas where female active articulation of sexual drives is still, to some extent, allowed. In modern cultures, Arthurs explains, where the codes of bodily decorum "demand of 'respectable' women an even greater restraint than men in the expression of spontaneous bodily desires" (142), humor provides women with a space "where the unthinkable and the undoable can be thought and done without retribution either from society in general or the individual psyche" (141). Arthurs's comments appear to be relevant to the way Asís employs irony regarding Pacheco's clothing. In addition to preventing her "confessors" from taking her indecorum too seriously (i.e., acknowledging and exploring her sexual desire), the irony stemming from the seemingly trivial-sounding topic allows Pardo Bazán's character to do *the unthinkable and undoable* for a woman of her class. It allows her to destabilize the prevailing notions of feminine propriety by questioning, and ultimately leaving to her audience's reconsideration, the logic (or rather the lack thereof) on which these notions are based: "Señor, ¿por qué no han de tener las mujeres derecho para encontrar guapos a los hombres que lo sean, y por qué ha de mirarse mal que lo manifiesten (aunque para manifestarlo dijesen tantas majaderías como los chulos del café Suizo)?" (93–94).

The protagonist's caution and constant awareness of others' scrutiny of her outward appearance also are evident in the part of the novel told by the external (and presumed masculine) narrator. "Luego las fiestecitas, los bailes ... que obligan a ir provisto de trajes de sociedad, porque si uno se presenta sencillo, de seda cruda, les choca y se ofenden y critican" (237), the narrator tells us about the marquesa's alertness to the society's vigilance and expectations. Also, the description of Asís's daydreams of traveling to Galicia, in which she devotes a great deal of attention to the nuances of her outfit, suggests that even in "una especie de somnambulismo" (275) she strives to comply with society's good taste: "Encontrábase ya en el vagón ... el velo de gasa inglesa bien ceñido sobre la toca de paja, calzados los guantes de camino, abrochado hasta el cuello el guardapolvo" (276). However, the portraits of Asís in which she conforms to the societal dress code are not the only images of her in the narrator's account. In addition to providing readers with conventional depictions of the main character in public, in which, as we have seen, bereft of bodily features, buttoned up, veiled, gloved (in short, confined to her outfit) she appears as a commodity, the narrator offers different images of her in private. Consider, for instance, the portrayal of Asís at home when Pacheco surprises her with his visit.

> No estaba Asís lo que se llamaba hecha un pingo, con traje roto y zapatos viejos ... su bata de chiné blanco tenía manchas y visos obscuros ... su peinado, revuelto sin arte, con rabos y mechones saliendo por aquí y por acullá, parecía obra de peluquería gatuna. (238–39)

Similar to the title of Pardo Bazán's short story *El encaje roto* (published two years before *Insolación*), which emblematizes, in Joyce Tolliver's words, the author's "simultaneous fabrication and destruction of conventional images of femininity" (*Cigar Smoke* 78), the details related to the deficiencies in Asís's apparel and hairstyle mark the narrator's defiance of the idealized modes of representing a nineteenth-century upper-class woman in a domestic sphere (López Fernández 58–77). By opening her door (inadvertently or not) to Pacheco while carelessly dressed and by bringing to his view what good taste dictates she should have kept private, the protagonist not only disregards nineteenth-century distinctions between private and public spheres. She also sabotages the convention that, as Tolliver put it, "privileges the public presentation of self over the expression of individual, private character" (*Cigar Smoke* 74). Significant in this context is also the focus on Asís's untidy hairdo. Given the recurrent nineteenth-century association between a woman's unruly hair and her unrestrained sexual energy (Bornay 56–67), it is evident that the narrator makes use of the symbolic value of the protagonist's jumbled hair to contest the romanticized image of a bourgeois woman not only in terms of her external appearance. Through the depiction of Asís's hair, the narrator also challenges the notion of her as a sexually passive being.

In the study of images of women in the nineteenth- and early-twentieth-century Spanish press, Adolfo Perinat and María Isabel Marrades comment:

> El pelo ... suelto que simboliza la sexualidad desenfrenada ... es algo sólo permitido en la intimidad más absoluta ... o antes de los 17 años. ... Pero pasada esa feliz edad, la mujer tiene que domeñar su pelo, recogerlo, alisarlo, cubrirlo y hacerlo pasar tan desapercibido como su propia sexualidad. (127)

Prompt in pointing out to readers the main character's efforts to uphold the societal status quo by imitating other ladies' stylish coiffures and striving to keep (at least for a while) her hairdo elegant and orderly, the narrator initially attributes the liability to Pacheco for getting the marquesa's hair messy. "Pacheco ocultó la cara en el pelo de la señora, descomponiéndolo y echándole el sombrero hacia atrás. Ella se lo arregló antes de llamar" (215), the narrator tells us shortly before offering another scene with don Diego loosening Asís's hairdo. "Aseveró esto metiendo sus dedos ... entre el pelo de la señora, y complaciéndose en alborotar el peinado sobrio ... que Asís trataba de imitar del de la Pinogrande, maestra en los toques de la elegancia" (221). It is tempting to assume that by providing these conventional scenes in which Asís and her suitor fulfill the roles that society has established for them (he actively pursuing his erotic desire, as indicated by the selection of verbs in both examples, while she merely reacts to it), the narrator attempts to protect the protagonist's good name. However, it is obvious (given the subsequent references to her hair) that he brings up the traditional pattern of female sexual conduct mostly to confront it. Consider once more, the depiction of the main character's hairdo when she is visited unexpectedly by don Diego ("su peinado, revuelto sin arte, con rabos y mechones saliendo por aquí y por acullá ..." [239]) and a subsequent similar image in the concluding episode ("Asís, despeinada, alegre, más fresca que el amanecer ..." [289]). If, indeed, as Galia Ofek asserts in her study of the erotic value of unruly female coiffure and its frequent deployment in nineteenth-century literature and paintings, "'sexual intimacy' was demonstrated 'by the undressed state of the woman's hair'" (66), then the narrator's description of Asís's uncontainable, rebellious hair aptly conveys her rejection of the societally imposed passivity. As the widow opens the door for Pacheco, her unruly hair foreshadows the course of action she will take when dealing with her desire. In addition, the marquesa's discomposed hairdo in the final scene denotes her premarital intimacy with Pacheco. After all, it is hardly a coincidence that the narrative voice opts for portraying Asís, to borrow Barbara Zecchi's words, "sin arreglo alguno ... despeinada y sonriente" (302), precisely at the moment in which she challenges "—con su gesto de 'ventanera'—la moral tradicional al exponer y enseñar al espacio público una trasgresión cometida entre las paredes domésticas" (Zecchi 302–03). Remarkably, however, it is not so much the tousled hair itself, as the narrator's reference to it *in conjunction with* the adjectives *alegre* and *fresca* that further stresses the protagonist's defiant attitude toward the customary standards of female sexual behavior. The choice of words points to enjoyment and satisfaction, which are things that a respectable nineteenth-century woman was not supposed to derive from such an experience and certainly never to reveal beyond her domestic walls.[8]

That the third-person narrator proves to be as skillful as Asís in manipulating and exploiting sartorial images to reaffirm and simultaneously challenge the patriarchal notion of femininity and that his references to the protagonist's *toilette* activities are as infused with ambivalence and irony as the main character's account itself is perhaps best in such seemingly trivial scenes as the marquesa's application of beauty products. Take, for example, the depiction of the bath and the preparation for it in chapter 10.

> Mientras no estaba dispuesto el baño, practicó Asís las operaciones de aseo que deben precederle: limpiarse y limarse las uñas ... registrarse ... las orejas con la esponjita y la cucharita de marfil, frotarse el pescuezo con el guante de crin suavizado con pasta de almendra y miel. ... Jabón y más jabón. Ahora agua de Colonia. ... (166–67)

One could read this scene as upholding the patriarchal status quo, since it recaptures, through so many details, the fervor with which Asís undertakes her cleansing procedures to strengthen her moral resolve. "In scrubbing her skin with such exasperated determination," notes Noël Valis, "the protagonist is obeying middle-class moral hygiene, demonstrating rigid self-control, and repressing her sexuality" ("Confession" 249). Alternatively, judging by the tone applied here, one could interpret this scene as the narrator's way of questioning the validity of the link between bodily cleanliness and feminine decorum. Given the irony in the description of the marquesa striving to see what is apparently problematic to see (as the presence of the verbs *creía ver* instead of *veía, confundía, juzgaba*, implies), the narrator doubts the effect of her cleansing operations on her moral strength. Ironically, the stronger Asís's determination to overcome her attraction to Pacheco, the more she scrubs her body and the more beauty products she applies, the more her actions seem to attest to the vigor of her erotic impulses. Similarly, the narrator's manipulation of the narrative perspective, evident in his switching from seeking at first to assert discursive authority to weakening it later, points to his wish to make visible the existence of Asís's desire and to exonerate himself from any accountability for doing so. Consider, once more, the narrator's description of the bathroom scene. In providing such a meticulous depiction of the marquesa's cleansing operations, the narrator asserts his discursive authority over the secrets of her *toilette* and, by extension, of her sexuality. However, just as the narrator is eager to emphasize his privileged knowledge of the protagonist's grooming activities, he is equally keen to reduce the liability for the presentation of this episode. He does so, by resorting to Asís's inner thoughts at its culminating point: "Agua clara y tibia —pensaba Asís—, lava, lava tanta grosería, tanto flamenquismo, tanta barbaridad: lava la osadía, lava el desacato, lava el aturdimiento, lava el ..." (167). In turning to Asís's inner deliberations, precisely in the middle of her most feverish attempts to wash off the dust and dirt from the fair, the narrator surely adds a dramatic element to this scene. More importantly, however, by switching from overtly deploring the marquesa's private moments to merely transcribing her thoughts, the narrator succeeds in lessening his accountability for exposing, in Jane Arthurs's phrase, "the potent mixture of disgust and desire" (140) that Asís associates with her adventure and the filth from the fair.

The mixed feeling of repulsion and desire that Pardo Bazán's protagonist experiences is hardly odd considering the importance that the nineteenth-century middle and upper classes placed on the maintenance of bodily decorum and the contempt and disgust to which they subjected anyone who broke the rules of *civilized* behavior (Arthurs 138–41). It is during the nineteenth century, asserts Arthurs, when the progressive marginalization of the carnival took place and the unrestrained indulgence in the pleasure of the body became increasingly linked to the subordinated culture of masses. Significantly, "the exclusion of carnival ... from the polite, legitimate culture of the bourgeoisie" (140), affirmed Arthurs, "did not do away with the desires which carnival expressed" (140). As the American scholar, Jerry Palmer, explains:

> The repression of the boisterous margin goes hand in hand with an unconscious desire for exactly the activities which are being repressed, and the more they are subjected to this marginalisation and repression, the more tainted they are with the "dirt" of their origins, the more attractive they become ... those who adhere to respectable morality are obliged to condemn what they most want and want what they most condemn. (qtd. in Arthurs 140)

Of course, neither Asís's attraction to the fair nor the connection between the wild atmosphere of the festivities and the marquesa's repressed sexuality escaped critics' attention (Valis, "Confession" 252–54). "When Asís attempts to wash off the dust and dirt of the fair," wrote Valis, "she re-enacts those repressed sexual desires that are associated, consciously or not, with the lower orders and dangerous elements of the fair" ("Confession" 256). However, it is also the emphasis on Asís's determination (reinforced by the array of cosmetics) with which she scrubs her body and the vehemence (intensified by the use of imperatives and the repetitions of words) with which she chastises what she enjoyed only a day before, that is vital here. For, it is her exaggerated determination that makes it possible for the narrator to imply that the protagonist, to borrow Palmer's words, "condemns what she most wants and wants what she most condemns," and to expose, in this way, the strength of her repressed desires.

The sartorial portrait of Asís makes manifest in sum that fashion provided Pardo Bazán with an effective medium to question the prevailing notions of femininity. By creating a character that upholds and, simultaneously, subverts, via her elegant *toilettes*, the patriarchal norms of feminine conduct, the author brought to light the ambivalent and changing nature of Spanish womanhood. By manipulating the sartorial images to affirm Asís's sexual desire, moreover, the writer explored a new model of feminine behavior and experimented (beneath the protective coverage of irony and ambivalence) with the traditional limits of femininity.

While challenging the boundaries of traditional womanhood and exploring a new model of feminine conduct was no doubt a bold move on Pardo Bazán's part, equally daring was her endeavor to redefine the limits of conventional femininity by suggesting amendments to the normative masculine role. As we shall see shortly in doña Emilia's portrayal of Asís's suitor Diego Pacheco, the novelist used her knowledge of men's fashion to do more than just bring to light the contradictions and ambiguities in the allegedly stable notion of nineteenth-century manhood in Spain. If changes to a woman's place in society were to occur in order for Spain to gain full entry into modernity, such a goal was reachable only through the reconfiguration of the existing paradigms of the masculine role and the acceptance of innovative, forward-looking models of masculinity.

Chapter Four

The Sartorial Charm of the Modern Man in Pardo Bazán's *Insolación*

In chapter 21 of Emilia Pardo Bazán's *Insolación* (1889), Gabriel Pardo confirms his suspicion that a male accessory, an English wallet, which he spotted some time earlier in the apartment of his friend the beautiful widow, Asís Taboada, marquesa de Andrade, belongs to her new lover, Diego Pacheco. Pardo's subsequent encounter with the young man in the marquesa's house, with the wallet in the Andalusian's hands, and "la ojeada expresiva que trocaron Pacheco y Asís" (280) during his visit, makes the lady's choice obvious to Gabriel. Yet, what remains unclear to him are the reasons why Asís, a woman who until now Pardo "creía una señora impecable" (210), decided on her new beau. The Galician artillery commander, whom the novelist seems to describe as the paragon of bourgeois respectability, wonders resentfully, "¡Cómo escogen las mujeres!" (281). Given Pardo's interest in the elegant and well-bred widow, his dislike of her suitor is self-explanatory. After all, as the narrator tells us, "raro es que el amigo de una dama, en caso semejante, no desapruebe la elección" (281). Yet Pardo's thoughts and resentment of the rival merit further examination since they resemble the disapproval expressed by the novel's first critics of Pacheco. "Pacheco es un imbécil de Sevilla, que a los que no nos enamoramos de las personas porque tengan las sienes algo cóncavas, no nos parece más que un revulsivo confitado" (1469), wrote Leopoldo Alas (Clarín) in his 1890 article, "Emilia Pardo Bazán y sus últimas obras." In addition to calling the gallant "andaluz de pastaflora" (1469) and "andalucito bobalicón y chorlito" (1474), Clarín further vented his contempt for doña Emilia's protagonist and his love affair as follows:

> Hay en todos los amores de estos dos, para el lector, una sensación semejante a la de estar comiendo huevos hilados, secos,

> todo el día, o mazapán de Toledo con sabor a la caja, o bizcochón viejo ... En fin, yo no sé cómo decirlo, pero *El cisne de Vilamorta* era un terrón de sal comparado con este Pachecazo que tanta gracia le hace a doña Asís la viuda. ... (1469)

Contemporary critics did not share (at least not to the same degree) Clarín's hostility toward Pacheco. At the same time, however, they did not find him worthy of profound analysis. Whereas most scholars focused on Pardo Bazán's representation of Asís Taboada, few critics devoted their attention to the author's portrait of Pacheco.[1] Described time and time again as well-dressed, idle, and sexy, doña Emilia's gallant was identified as the embodiment of the nineteenth-century *señorito* (Ortiz 51–52), a predecessor of the New Man (Charnon-Deutsch, *Narratives of Desire* 167–68), and a caricature version of don Juan Tenorio (Zecchi 299–300). Most recently, Pacheco's stylish outfits and nonchalant attitude have linked him to a "peculiar brand of dandyism" (Amann 185).[2] However, as these studies indicate, Pardo Bazán's portrayal of don Diego is far more problematic than it appears at first sight. Even though the fashionable Andalusian undeniably assimilates various characteristics commonly associated with the nineteenth-century *señorito*, the New Man, the Don Juan, and the dandy, he never fully resembles any one of these types of men.

In what follows, I will examine the aspect of Pacheco that has attracted some attention from critics, but has not been, as of yet, adequately explored: his sartorial charm. More specifically, I will demonstrate how Pardo Bazán made use of her male protagonist's fashionable clothing and accessories to imbue his portrait with contradictions and ambiguities that ultimately allowed her to bring to light incoherencies in the allegedly stable notion of nineteenth-century middle- and upper-class manhood in Spain. Rather than link Pacheco to any specific stereotype of a nineteenth-century male, I will reveal the author used her knowledge of men's fashion not only to point out her protagonist's adherence and transgression of the gender norms, but also, and perhaps more importantly, to present her readers with an alternative construction of the masculine role.

Before delving into the sartorial representation of Pacheco, it may be useful to look at Pardo Bazán's comments on men's fashion. Although the novelist wrote less and not as frequently about the male art of dressing as she did on women's fashion, the detailed observations and examples that she provided in her essays to denounce the ugliness and discomfort of a gentleman's wardrobe show that she was not a novice in this subject matter. For instance, in "Más indumentaria," an article that Pardo Bazán wrote in *El Imparcial* a year after she published *Insolación*, the writer criticized men's style of dressing by describing the unaesthetic ("los pantalones tan feísimos" [1]), the ridiculous ("¿Dónde se habrán dejado todos los detractores del ropaje masculino su parte más risible ... nuestra *chistera*?" [1; Pardo Bazán's italics]), and uncomfortable features of specific clothing items.[3] In addition, in her subsequent essays, "la vestimenta masculina le pareció con frecuencia absurda" (Ruíz-Ocaña Dueñas 375). In "La vida en verano. —Cuestión de ropa: San Lorenzo mártir" (1900), for example, doña Emilia called attention to the aspects of male attire that were inappropriate for the season and wondered why men "han de conservar a toda costa la corrección de la indumentaria" (538) and "bajo temperaturas de África han de ir con su cuello tieso y su ropa de paño" (538).[4]

Of course, unattractiveness and the lack of comfort were not the only features of the male wardrobe that Pardo Bazán censured in her articles. In addition to disapproving of the conservative and unappealing qualities of specific clothing items, she repeatedly criticized the docility with which men submitted to the inflexible rules of dressing.[5] However, if men held on so tightly to their dressing etiquette and did not protest against the dullness of their clothing, even though, as doña Emilia observed, they did not enjoy wearing it ("Se me objetará que los hombres se hallan a gusto con su vestimenta. Lo niego" ["Más indumentaria" 1]), then the reason for it, perhaps, was that they feared any perceptible changes to the supposedly stable ideals of masculinity. Given nineteenth-century Spanish society's obsession and inflexibility with gender boundaries and the common perception that "men concerned with fashion [were] not really men at all, but effeminate dandies" (McKinney 96), it should not come as a surprise that a typical bourgeois male would sacrifice his comfort and aesthetic taste rather than venture to display care for his external appearance. Doing otherwise, would expose him to the risk of acquiring unmanly qualities and crossing the limits of his gender.

It is, of course, not a coincidence that Pardo Bazán's article "Más indumentaria" is written as a reply to a letter from an anonymous, allegedly male reader from Coria, who brushes aside the idea of women wearing divided skirts in public. Even the thought

Chapter Four

that the opposite sex could adopt any aspect of male clothing makes the reader feel, as doña Emilia ironically put it, "un poquillo alarmado" ("Más indumentaria" 1), fretful of "la confusión que vendría a establecerse si hembras y varones usasen indistintamente el mismo traje" ("Más indumentaria" 1), and resentful of any amendments to the established gender norms. However, if irony, which pervades the tone of doña Emilia's response, is indicative of anything, then assuring the reader that her comments will not have much effect on everyday customs (i.e., on women's or men's ways of dressing), does not merely reflect the rigid nature of gender norms but brings forward the novelist's critique of them.

> Tranquilícese el lector cauriense … que no conviene alarmarse por artículo mas o menos, aunque en esos artículos se pretenda modificar rancias costumbres, al parecer inalterables. Hágase cargo de que, cuando atacamos *costumbres*, dirigimos el tiro contra ideas; y con las ideas ocurre lo que con los astros; a veces, después que ya no existen, aún nos llega su luz por espacio de siglos: así se perpetúan en costumbres actuales ideas difuntas ya, sin que lo note el mismo que las acata. … no crea tanto en la eficacia de la pluma para trastornar de golpe los ejes de la sociedad ni … para modificar el rumbo de la indumentaria. ("Más indumentaria" 1; Pardo Bazán's italics)

As one can see, while downplaying the influence of her pen, Pardo Bazán censured the stagnant nature of cultural values (as the choice of words: *rancias*, *inalterables*, *difuntas*, indicates) and the obliviousness of those who adhere to them. The part of the sentence, in fact, "sin que lo note el mismo que las acata," carries the strongest criticism on Pardo Bazán's part of those (and as the presence of "el mismo" would suggest, she meant men) who never seem to question the rationality of rules laid down by the patriarchal system. By accepting these rules (whether with respect to dressing, gendered behavior, or otherwise) as standards, men perpetuate them blindly. It is why, Pardo Bazán explained years later, "se me figura que las modas no ejercen tanta influencia como se supone en las costumbres, que los ojos se habitúan a todo" (*Crónicas de Europa* 688). She further elaborated this statement by giving an example in which even the most preposterous manner of dressing, once assimilated in everyday life, becomes a cultural norm: "la mujer salvaje, sin otra ropa que un cinturón, ni escandaliza ni solivianta al hombre de su tribu con mayor intensidad que si estuviese toda engaritada en esteras o pieles de animales" (*Crónicas de Europa* 688). However, we should not take too literally the author's comments in *Crónicas de Europa* or her conclusions in the reply to her reader from Coria.[6] It is true that the image of bourgeois Spaniards stubbornly clinging to the established patterns of dressing was not a promising sign for change in the cultural ideals of manhood in the near future in Spain. Nevertheless, the supposed lack of advancement in men's attire in real life did not prevent doña Emilia from resorting to the language of fashion in her narrative to form a dialogue with existing perspectives on gender order. As the depictions of Pacheco's stylishness in *Insolación* indicate, the art of dressing provided Pardo Bazán with an effective medium to challenge the patriarchal gender ideology. Similar to the way in which the novelist deployed a variety of sartorial details to push the parameters of gender order in her portrait of Asís, she used her knowledge of men's art of dressing to shed light on Pacheco's manners of crossing and recrossing the limits of his gender and on the inconsistencies in the dominant ideals of masculinity. Long before Pardo Bazán visited the 1900 World Exhibition in Paris where she identified fashion as a creative force behind the new gender identity ("En estos diecinueve siglos ha sido creada la mujer" [*Cuarenta días en la Exposición* 237]), the novelist already made use of her male protagonist's voguish outfits in *Insolación* to explore new models of masculine conduct. By resorting to the allegedly unchanging features of male dressing etiquette, the author managed to fill her depictions of Pacheco with contradictions and ambiguities that in the end enabled her to challenge the supposedly stable notions of manhood in Spain and to create, as we will see, her own vision of a modern man.

Details of Pacheco's sartorial charm abound in *Insolación*. "El galán venía todo soplado, con una camisa y un chaleco como el ampo de la nieve, el ojal guarnecido de fresquísimo clavel, guantes de piel de perro flamantitos y, en suma, todas las señales de haberse acicalado mucho" (239), the narrator tells us for instance in chapter 17. However, while it is tempting to assume that these features have an effect, as Elizabeth Scarlett maintains, of "establishing the mannequinlike figure of Pacheco, who is what he wears" (35), the portrayal of the protagonist is anything but unproblematic. As one can notice in Asís's and the third-person narrator's respective

Chapter Four

accounts, even the seemingly innocuous references to Pacheco's finery and the manner in which he carries himself in his wardrobe point to the ways in which the elegant suitor conforms to and, concomitantly, moves away from the conventional model of masculinity. Consider, for example, Asís's first depiction of don Diego at the *tertulia* in chapter 2. By dressing conservatively, that is, by wearing what any nineteenth-century gentleman who was well-versed in dressing etiquette would wear for such an occasion (i.e., a *frac*), Pacheco (who also appears reticent, serious, and guarded in sharing his opinions) successfully embodies the ideal of a respectable young man. Also by equipping himself with a watch—a symbol for reliability, regularity, and promptness—the protagonist reinforces the image of a proper young man. Yet, meeting the sartorial expectation alone does not necessarily testify to the Andalusian's adherence to the hegemonic gender ideology of his time. With his manner of wearing the *frac* "con soltura" (83) together with his airs of Englishness, Pacheco singles himself out during the *tertulia*. In this way, he exhibits behavior that already prior to the nineteenth century members of his class considered improper for his gender.[7] Also the use of the word—*frac*—is significant to the initial portrait of Pacheco. Because the *frac*, as Radana Strbáková asserts, stood originally for "'hábito de fraile' y 'bata de mujer o de niño'" (885), the depiction of don Diego in his frock coat links him to women and the image of a child in that it goes along with the duquesa de Sahagún's description of him as a womanizer ("lo único para que hasta la fecha servía era para trastornar la cabeza a las mujeres" [90]) and conveniently corroborates her portrayal of him as an immature man.

> La Sahagún … añadió que ahí donde lo veíamos, hecho un moro por la indolencia y un inglés por la sosería, no era sino un calaverón de tomo y lomo … muy gastador y muy tronera, de quien su padre no podía hacer bueno, ni traerle al camino de la formalidad y del sentido práctico. … (90)[8]

Examples of the protagonist's simultaneous adherence and non-adherence to the norms of conventional masculinity also are manifest in Asís's straightforward and yet ambiguous depictions of don Diego in the subsequent chapter. Take, for instance, the marquesa's account of her admirer's application of hair lotion:

The Sartorial Charm of the Modern Man

> Introduje el rabo postizo de la flor en el ojal de Pacheco, y tomando de mi corpiño un alfiler sujeté la gardenia, cuyo olor a pomada me subía al cerebro, mezclado con otro perfume fino, procedente, sin duda, del pelo de mi acompañante. Sentí un calor extraordinario en el rostro, y al levantarlo, mis ojos se tropezaron con los del meridional, que en vez de darme las gracias, me contempló de un modo expresivo e interrogador. En aquel momento casi me arrepentí de la humorada de ir a la feria; pero ya ... (101)

Given the negative attitude toward men's application of cosmetics in the nineteenth-century bourgeois culture (Fuentes Peris 51–52), it is obvious that Pardo Bazán's protagonist does not concern himself too much with conforming to the image of a "real" man. Although delicate, the lotion is strong enough for Asís to identify ("perfume fino, procedente, sin duda, del pelo de mi acompañante" [101]) and to experience its effects: "Sentí un calor extraordinario" (101). At the same time, however, the Andalusian's refusal to be the marquesa's object of olfactory delight falls in line with the traditional pattern of masculine behavior. By reclaiming the position of gazing subject, that is, as Collin McKinney explains, "a (masculine) position of power" (85) and by conveying his disapproval of Asís's conduct ("me contempló de un modo expresivo e interrogador" [101]) Pacheco succeeds in keeping his masculinity intact.

Yet, the problematic relation to the established norms of masculinity is not all that Asís's references to her suitor's finery bring forward in her account. As the widow's description as well as her attitude toward Pacheco's external presentation before and during the trip to the fair suggest, the marquesa uses the features of the Andalusian's sartorial charm to challenge the patriarchal model of masculinity by presenting an alternative version of a masculine role. Consider the appearance of don Diego before the trip to the fair in his three-piece, gray suit and with a cigar—an emblem of traditional masculinity par excellence—in his hand. The widow tells us straightforwardly that Pacheco's attire was appealing to her: "En suma, Pacheco, que vestía un elegante terno gris claro, me pareció galán de veras" (94). Curiously, however, it is her detailed account of her suitor in the same outfit, but this time, with his hat off, his hair disheveled, and his partially unbuttoned shirt at the fair, that discloses her veneration and endorsement of Pacheco's unconventional way of being. What attracts the marquesa to her companion, in other words, is that his behavior (as her depiction of his wardrobe implies) proves to be more relaxed in terms of social entanglements and rules of dressing etiquette:

>   —¡Qué bonitos ojos azules tiene este perdis! —pensaba yo para mí.
>   El gaditano estaba sin sombrero; vestía un traje ceniza, elegante, de paño rico y flexible; de vez en cuando se enjugaba la frente sudorosa con un pañuelo fino, y a cada movimiento se le descomponía el pelo ... parecía doblemente morena su tez ... porque hacia la parte que ya cubre el cuello de la camisa se entreveía un cutis claro. (124)

Given that the sartorial charm of a nineteenth-century gentleman rested not only in his way of dressing, but also in his manners, gestures, and bearing, significant are also Asís's comments on her admirer's demeanor. "Para llegar adonde yo indicaba, era preciso saltar un vallado, bastante alto por más señas. Pacheco lo salvó y desde el lado opuesto me tendió los brazos" (145), the marquesa tells us. We might think, of course, that don Diego's physical prowess is what mesmerizes Asís the most here. Male physical strength was, after all, a quality that the social commentator Mariano Carderera y Potó listed in his *Diccionario de Pedagogía* (1854), alongside "la robustez ... las fuerzas corporales y el poder de la inteligencia" (qtd. in Espigado Tocino 137), as highly estimable in a nineteenth-century Spanish male. However, in truth, even though there could be no doubt that Asís's feasts her eyes on her companion's physical fitness (as she does many times during their outings together) she relishes, at the same time, equally, if not more, his acquiescence to her dictating ("Para llegar *adonde yo indicaba*" [145; my italics]) his course of action.

In her study on gender roles in eighteenth- and nineteenth-century Spain, Bridget Aldaraca asserts "the virtue of feminine docility or submissive behavior [was], in the male, diagnosed as illness" (*El Ángel del Hogar* 215). Thus, because "to cede one's will to another in order to please contradict[ed] the model of patriarchal masculinity" (Aldaraca, *El Ángel del Hogar* 215), this characteristic of Pacheco in Asís's narrative might come across (as it did to the novel's first critic [i.e., Clarín]) as a sign of the protagonist's emasculation. As Carderera y Potó claimed in his 1854 *Diccio-*

nario de Pedagogía, "un hombre que crea merecer dicho apelativo jamás deberá ser ... sensible, afectuoso ... cordial ... paciente" (qtd. in Espigado Tocino 138). Hence, don Diego, who on more than one occasion exhibits these traits, strays from the traditional pattern of masculine behavior. However, as one can tell from the widow's affirmative reaction to Pacheco's transgression of sartorial rules and, in particular, from her marveling at the gallant's supposedly inappropriate, unmanly features (i.e., his hat off and his unbuttoned shirt in public), emasculation is not the purpose of Asís's alternative image of don Diego. Because a hat was an accessory that in the nineteenth-century culture "[stood] for that very organ which men feared to lose" (Garb 38), the marquesa draws attention to its absence on Pacheco's head and to his shirt (which, while unbuttoned, makes him an object of scrutiny) to expand the accepted norms of an upper-class man for presenting himself in public. In doing so, the marquesa enriches the image of don Diego with characteristics that in the past society did not attribute in a positive manner to masculine behavior. Through those seemingly insignificant details, thus, she ventures to sketch an alternative ideal of a bourgeois man.

That the details of Pacheco's sartorial charm provide efficient means to question the patriarchal notions of masculinity is also evident from the role they play in suffusing Asís's narrative with ironic effects. As Christina Karageorgou-Bastea shows, irony is used in the depiction of almost all characters in *Insolación* and it originates from the contradictions between their words and deeds (235–37). It is the irony, asserts Karageorgou-Bastea, through which the narrative voice "desacredita la presencia de un único punto de vista ... relativiza lo que en apariencia fue afirmado 'rotundamente'" (241). These comments also are pertinent to the part of the novel told from Asís's perspective in that, as in the third-person narrator's account, irony makes relative what appears to be certain in the widow's narrative and enables her to voice her critique of gender conventions. However, in Asís's account, irony stems not only from the incongruity between the protagonists' words and acts. As one can see from the marquesa's aforementioned description of don Diego with a cigar in his hand at the beginning of chapter 3, it originates also from the disparity between deeply embedded cultural meanings attached to masculine accoutrements and men's application of them. "Poco distaba

Chapter Four

ya de la iglesia, cuando distinguí a un caballero, que parado al pie de corpulento plátano, arrojaba a los jardines un puro enterito y se dirigía luego a saludarme" (93). Critics have observed that in Pardo Bazán's short stories "¿Cobardía?" (1891) and "La punta del cigarro" (1914) the respective narrators capitalized on readers' conventional association with such an iconic hallmark of masculinity as a cigar to rewrite the traditional gender roles (Hoffman, "Of Broken Fans" 401–09) and to question (beneath the protective covering of irony) their rationality (Tolliver, *Cigar Smoke* 79–104; McKenna 109–23). Asís's reference to this particular paraphernalia in Pacheco's hand serves an analogous purpose. In drawing attention to her suitor's cigar, the marquesa affirms his virility. At the same time, however, by pointing to the Andalusian throwing away the *entire* cigar precisely before meeting her, the widow uses the irony that stems from the discrepancy between conventional expectations of masculine conduct and Pacheco's actions, not only to tease her audience with hinting at the possibility of the gallant's willingness to surrender his manliness. By playing with readers' assumptions, she also calls into question the validity of gender-coded cultural clichés on which the standard ideals of bourgeois masculinity were based.[9]

Adherence and transgression of the existing gender paradigms are also at the heart of the third-person narrator's references to don Diego's sartorial appeal. Take, for instance, the narrator's ambivalent depiction of the protagonist's elegance in chapters 11 and 17. The portrayal of Pacheco in his pristine vest and shirt ("chaleco blanquísimo" [177]; "una camisa y un chaleco como el ampo de la nieve" [239]), and his "guantes de piel" (239), recalls Mesonero Romanos's description of a bourgeois male in *Memorias de un setentón* (1880), who in his "chaleco ... pechera y guante blanco, representab[a] ... la alta posición" (304). By placing emphasis on these items in Pacheco's appearance, the narrator points, in this manner, to his observance of the established dressing codes and his effort to embody through them the image of a perfect gentleman. Concurrently, however, by expanding the gallant's portrait with such clues as: "la elegancia no estudiada de su vestir" (177), "el ojal guarnecido de fresquísimo clavel" (239), and "las señales de haberse acicalado mucho" (239), in other words, features proper of a man of leisure, the narrator links him consciously also to the figure of the dandy.[10]

The Sartorial Charm of the Modern Man

"Diego's dandyism is clear ... in his ease, elegance and superficiality" (185–86), wrote Elizabeth Amann. Moreover, it is his playfulness that makes Asís feel "in the company of this dandy ... immune to gravity, to seriousness and depth" (Amann 186). However, given the nineteenth-century dandy's defiant position toward the dominant gender norms, his mocking attitude toward the "comfortable bourgeois notions of order" (Feldman 103), and the nature of the conversation between the marquesa and the protagonist in chapter 17, the evocation of this figure in the third-person narrator's account is significant also for another reason. The description of the Andalusian's external appearance that "brings to mind ... [the] archetype of the feminized aesthete" (Tsuchiya, *Marginal Subjects* 143) precisely in the scene in which he persuades the widow to break, once again, the rules of feminine decorum and meet with him alone at the outskirts of the city, enables the narrator to emphasize the protagonist's laissez-faire attitude toward the rules of courtship. Moreover, the violation of proper (for a gentleman) conduct in this scene in which the young man shows up unexpectedly at the marquesa's house at an unusual time ("¿Quién contaba con Pacheco a tales horas? [las diez y media de la mañana]" [238]), allows the narrator to use the protagonist's dandyism to accentuate his lax observance of the established norms of behavior. In doing so, the narrative voice similar to Asís, marks the fissures and contradictions in the allegedly solid, unitary model of middle- and upper-class manhood in Spain.

Pacheco's dandyism (even though he differs in many aspects, as Amann has noted, from the classic nineteenth-century dandy) is certainly not lost on the marquesa. Ultimately, however, it is not the suitor's affinity to this figure alone, but rather his ability to embody both—the image of the dandy and the gentleman—that fascinates the widow. What draws Asís to him, and what the third-person narrator conveys aptly through the language of clothing, is the ease with which the Andalusian upholds and, at the same time, breaks away from the traditional patterns of masculine conduct. Consider, for example, the narrator's reference to the protagonist's choice of wardrobe for his evening encounter with Asís in the opening sentence in chapter 16: "Era Pacheco, envuelto en su capa de embozos grana, impropia de la estación, y de hongo" (220). Of course, such a comment does not seem, at first blush, to

Chapter Four

point to anything unusual. As Pedro Antonio de Alarcón noted in his *Viajes por España* (1883), *la capa y el hongo* were the standard components of young men's outfits that they would wear to appear outside their fiancées' balconies or windows late at night. In the chapter entitled, "Todas las Granadinas pelan la pava," Alarcón explained:

> Sí, señor; lo mismo la hija del Marqués o del Conde, que la del médico o el abogado ... todas hablan con el novio por el balcón, por la reja ... Pegado a una reja ... hay un fantasma con capa y hongo. ... La capa y el hongo del galán contribuyen al equívoco, pues todas las capas y todos los hongos son iguales a media noche. (236–37)

Also in Leopoldo Alas's *La Regenta* (1885), Alvaro de Mesía (similar to Pacheco, as Gloria Ortiz pointed out) is described in Ana Ozores's thoughts "envuelto en una capa de embozos grana, cantando bajo los balcones de Rosina" (1: 227). Significantly, however, unlike Pardo Bazán's character, Clarín's suitor does not wear the same type of hat: *el hongo*. Bearing in mind the cultural history of *la capa* and *el hongo*, it is evident that the narrator's seemingly casual reference to these two items in Pacheco's wardrobe is far from incidental. *La capa*, which (except for its popularity during the 1889 World Exhibition in Paris) "se vio arrinconada por el gabán" (Pena González, *Traje* 238) during the early decades in Spain, was worn since the 1840s mostly by conservative Spaniards. In contrast *el hongo* (the bowler), which since the 1850s gradually succeeded *la chistera* (the top hat), was adopted by liberal men who were often rebellious toward social conventions.[11] Hence, in pointing out that the protagonist wears the traditional garb—a cape—right at the outset of chapter 16, the narrator seems to affirm that the suitor adheres perfectly to the rules of conduct by visiting Asís at night. Overall, Pacheco does what Gabriel Pardo did in chapter 13 and what the Galician commander has been accustomed to doing for some time now. "Solía el comandante Pardo ir alguna que otra noche a casa de ... la Marquesa de Andrade. Charlaban de mil cosas, disputando, acalorándose, y en suma, pasando la velada solos, contentos y entretenidos" (188). The southerner also behaves like a true gentleman in that he shows up at the lady's house, as the narrator dutifully reports, at a similar time ("Eran las nueve menos cuarto ... Se oyó un campanillazo"

[219]) as Pardo: "Serían las nueve cuando llamó a la puerta" (188). He also leaves the widow's place before midnight, as his rival did previously. Nevertheless, the narrator's employment of the Andalusian's cape is more ambivalent than it appears at first sight. While this traditional clothing item helps him to mark the suitor's observance of societal conventions, his description of the garment, conversely, enables him to cast doubt on don Diego's conservativism. By interjecting a phrase to depict Pacheco's *capa* as "impropia de la estación" (220) directly after drawing attention to the marquesa's efforts to send her servants away before the meeting in the preceding chapter, the narrator manages to suggest that the gallant wears his cape not so much to exhibit his adherence to tradition, but to protect his identity. Thus, his decision to don the cape hints at the possibility that his encounter with Asís is of a more intimate nature than society would permit.

Less ambivalent is the narrator's use of the symbolic value of the second component of Pacheco's outfit: his hat. Like most nineteenth-century real-life men and literary characters who would opt for wearing *el hongo* instead of *la chistera*, Asís's suitor does not make much of a secret of his divergence from the traditional notions of masculinity.[12] A man should "ambicionar lo que no tiene, jamás contentarse con la posición que ocupa," wrote Carderera y Potó in his *Diccionario de Pedagogía* (qtd. in Espigado Tocino 138). Additionally, he should practice moderation in sexual activities, since an excess in them poses a threat to his virility, as Monlau warned in *Higiene del matrimonio o El libro de los casados*.[13] So, while calling attention to Pacheco's self-proclaimed lack of ambition ("Mi padre, empeñao ... que me meta en política ... y vaya ... al Congreso ... ¡En el Congreso yo!" [227]) and his bragging about the number of his sexual conquests ("Yo galanteé a trescientas mil mujeres" [225]) the narrator succeeds in portraying Asís's gallant as a man who does credit to the type of hat he wears and openly resists the limits of normative masculinity.

Yet, as in the marquesa's account, the third-person narrator's references to Pacheco's wardrobe convey more than the suitor's concurrent adherence and resistance to the existing gender norms. For the narrator, too, proves to be as skillful as Asís in manipulating the features of Pacheco's sartorial elegance to defy the patriarchal ideals of masculinity by reconfiguring its limits and exploring an alternative version of the masculine role. Consider once more

Chapter Four

the depiction of the protagonist in his cape and a bowler. By choosing to describe the gallant precisely in an outfit that combines the traditional Spanish garment with the avant-garde, foreign clothing item, the narrator provides his audience with an image of a man who is at ease with blending and blurring the conventional and the modern. What the narrator appreciates the most in Pacheco, however, is that he is capable of combining these two categories not only in his manner of dress, but also, and perhaps more importantly (as the marquesa's mental portrait of him indicates fittingly at the end of the same chapter), in his way of being.

> Llegada a este capítulo, la dama se dedicó a recordar ... lindo mosaico de gracias y méritos de su adorador. ... su rara mezcla de espontaneidad popular y cortesía hidalga; sus rasgos calaverescos y humorísticos unidos a cierta hermosa tristeza romántica. ... (233–34)

Equally telling is the seemingly insignificant episode of Pacheco's putting on Asís's slipper:

> Saltó Asís ... muerta de risa, y al saltar perdió una de sus bonitas chinelas, que por ser sin talón, a cada rato se le escurrían del pie. Recogióla Pacheco, calzándosela con mil extremos y zalamerías. (229)

Through the portrayal of the protagonist placing a lady's clothing item on his foot, the narrator points to the Andalusian's challenging the boundaries of his gender by undermining the core distinction—the feminine versus the masculine—on which the bourgeois system of gender differentiation was/is based. Of course, "a male identification with the feminine" (93), as Rita Felski wrote with respect to the crisis of gender in the *fin-de-siècle* European (English, French, and German) culture, even though it enables the articulations of alternative constructions of gender, is not "*necessarily* subversive of patriarchal privilege" (93; Felski's italics). In fact, Felski argued, the male appropriation of the feminine often "reinscribes more insistently those gender hierarchies which are ostensibly being called into question" (92).

Felski's comments, although persuasive for the examples that she provided in her study, are hardly applicable in *Insolación*. Despite his transgressive gesture, Pacheco is not a cross-dresser, since, as Radana Strbáková demonstrates in a variety of nineteenth-century literary texts (749–50), *chinelas* were part of both women's and men's wardrobes. Additionally, if the description of the above-mentioned scene is taken at face value, it appears that the southerner puts Asís's slipper on with no intention of wearing it, but to entertain the lady he courts, in other words, with the purpose of having fun with it. Yet, the fact that the protagonist crosses the limits of masculine and feminine so free of care and that he exhibits no concern at all about what the appropriation of the feminine might imply in terms of his sexuality and gender identity points to an endeavor on the narrator's part of renegotiating the limits of Pacheco's gender. The narrator, like Asís, attempts to provide an image of an alternative type of masculinity. He ventures, in other words, to delineate a portrait of a bourgeois male who is more flexible and more relaxed with respect to the traditional gender distinctions.

Significant also in this context is the tone in which the narrator presents this episode. By describing don Diego putting on the feminine article of clothing as a playful, teasing act, the narrator prevents readers from any serious speculations regarding the gallant's gender identity and sexuality. The lighthearted atmosphere, furthermore, shields the narrator from readers' possible suspicion and arraignment of his endorsement of the protagonist's unbefitting behavior. However, humor (or, more precisely, Pacheco's self-parody, which, in fact, is the parody of the normative masculinity) covers as much as it reveals. While its presence lays bare the narrator's effort to circumvent the watchful gaze of his audience and, by extension, his awareness of readers' sensitivity and anxiety toward the end-of-the-century crisis of gender, it also reveals that Pacheco's mocking the limits of patriarchal masculinity has more to do with an attempt at reconfiguring these boundaries than reinforcing them. Transvestism, as Gilbert and Gubar have demonstrated, has been an effective narrative strategy to break down the conventional definitions of gender "from Shakespeare and Sidney on" (325) up to the twentieth century. The act of cross-dressing, however blameless it might appear, as well as the figure of cross dresser, whether presented as a ruse or not, seems to irreversibly construct a connection, to adopt Marjorie Garber's words, to "a crisis of 'category' … [a] space of anxiety about fixed and changing identities" (32). Hence, the element of self-parody

Chapter Four

in *Insolación*, which is manifest in the distortion of the image of a gentleman in the deceptively innocent, burlesque scene of Pacheco putting on the lady's slipper, aids Pardo Bazán's narrator not only to challenge, but also to explore, beneath its protective umbrella, ahead of the limits of the traditional ideals of masculinity.

To conclude, the sartorial depiction of Pacheco demonstrates that fashion was a fitting medium for Pardo Bazán to take issue with the patriarchal gender ideology and to contest the prevailing notion of masculinity as a unified whole, "a perfect construct," as the American scholar George Mosse put it, "where every part was in its place" (5). In using her knowledge of the male art of dressing to draw attention to Pacheco's adherence and transgression of the gender norms, the novelist did not merely bring to light the contradictions and ambiguities in the normative notions of masculinity. Through her clever manipulation of the elements of Pacheco's sartorial charm, doña Emilia also ventured to provide her audience with an alternative model of the masculine role.

Yet, similar to her portrait of Asís, in her depiction of Pacheco, Pardo Bazán did not limit her use of fashion to address merely gender issues. The writer's attempt to delineate via sartorial features the image of don Diego as a modern man suggests that in her eyes Spain's full entry into modernity required not only the redefinition of the feminine role but also the reconfiguration of the masculine one as well. By using the art of dressing to draw contours of a more desirable type of masculinity in close relation to the unconventional female subject, Pardo Bazán succeeded, moreover, in pointing out that finding new definitions for the feminine role would depend on the successful reshaping of the normative notions of masculinity. In other words, if the remodeling of current ideals of womanhood were to take place in order for Spain to truly advance with the process of modernization, changes to women's place in society could not happen without simultaneous amendments to the established paradigms of the masculine role.

Given Pardo Bazán's unveiled critique of Spanish men's insistence on preserving the status quo regarding woman's position in society and her disappointment with their unyieldingness concerning gender relations in general in "La mujer española" (86–87), it is apparent that fashion "acts as a vehicle for fantasy" (Wilson, *Adorned in Dreams* 246) in her portrayal of Pacheco in

Insolación. As Wilson maintains, to dress ourselves (or others) *à la mode* "is not to search for some aesthetically pleasing form of utilitarian dress [but] … rather … to express and explore our more daring aspirations" (*Adorned in Dreams* 247). Although the scholar's comment originates from a different cultural context, it is, nevertheless, illuminating concerning Pardo Bazán's use of the art of dressing in Pacheco's portrait. Even though in her description of don Diego as a modern man, doña Emilia envisioned many traits that in 1889 Spain were to remain in the sphere of feminist fantasy, by deploying fashionable details to demarcate an alternative type of masculinity, she created more than an image of a fashionable, good-looking man. By skillfully maneuvering the elements of the protagonist's sartorial allure, the novelist managed to explore and express her daring aspirations about what forms this alternative type of masculinity could take.

The positive image of Pacheco as an elegant, modern man allowed doña Emilia to address cultural anxieties related to the late-nineteenth-century crisis of gender. By creating a character, who with flair and effortlessness crosses and recrosses the limits of his gender and who, in doing so, not only retains, but also increases his masculine charm (and wins, in this way, his counterpart's affection), Pardo Bazán downplayed the patriarchal fears of a modern man as the embodiment of effeminacy and decadence (Tsuchiya, *Marginal Subjects* 112–35). Similar to her colleague, Jacinto Octavio Picón, who, as we will see in the next chapter, also availed himself of the symbolic value of clothing and accessories to delineate his own controversial vision of a New Woman, doña Emilia shed light on the instability of gender norms in an innovative manner. As Picón will do in *Dulce y sabrosa*, through the image of her stylish character, Pardo Bazán marked the need to rewrite the asymmetrical gender positions in Spain. Using the language of fashion, thus, she cajoled her audience to imagine, in a gratifying way, an alternative portrait of a bourgeois male and ventured to open up new possibilities for the cultural constructions of manhood as a part of the formation of modern Spain.

Chapter Five

Dressing the New Woman in Picón's *Dulce y sabrosa*

In "A quien leyere," a note to the reader in the first edition of *Dulce y sabrosa* (1891), Jacinto Octavio Picón asked his audience to receive his work "no como novela que mueve a pensar, sino como juguete novelesco, contraveneno del tedio y engañifa de las horas" (67). As if to reinforce the notion that the purpose of his writing was to entertain and not to moralize, he added "Advertencia para esta edición" to the 1909 edition of the novel. In it, the novelist presented his readers with the following: "No busques en mis cuentos y novelas lección ni enseñanza: quédese el adoctrinar para el docto, como el moralizar para el virtuoso: sólo tienes que agradecerme el empeño que puse en divertir y acortar tus horas de aburrimiento y tristeza" (66). As critics emphasized, Picón's novel was not consistent with his words in *Dulce y sabrosa* (Sobejano, "Introducción," *Dulce y sabrosa* 28–29; Mandrell 171–72; Yáñez 263). "[T]he novelist's claims to literary frivolity, real enough in his style and elegant wit" (143), commented Noël Valis, "are continually undermined by a half-hidden, sometimes open, intent to instruct and inform" (*The Novels of Picón* 143). Nevertheless, the author did deliver what he promised in the preface to his work. The elaborated portrait of the physically stunning and exquisitely dressed main character, Cristeta Moreruela, shows that Picón, by resorting to the language of fashion, described his female protagonist as the quintessence of sensual and sartorial beauty as if she, indeed, was created first and foremost for the delight of others.

The persistent use of fashionable details in Picón's depiction of Cristeta as well as in his portrayals of other female characters in his narrative did not escape scholarly attention (Valis, "The Female Figure" 302–05; Sobejano, "Introducción," *Dulce y sabrosa* 18–19; Miguel 129–30). "En las mujeres piconianas ... el vestido ... destaca por su sencillez y elegancia ... Ropas ajustadas,

Chapter Five

tejidos transparentes, escotes, ropa interior, calzado y sombrero, son elementos primordiales en el aderezo femenino y poderosos medios de seducción" (Ezama Gil, "El profeminismo" 174). More recently, Travis Landry drew attention to the richness of Cristeta's attire: "The adornments of the novel's female protagonist, Cristeta, act as a determinative factor in the sexual selection process" (143). Yet, Landry too limited the role of the main character's stylish garments to "her weapon of … conquest" (144) and mainly linked "the relationship between Cristeta and her manner of dress [to] … her malleability as a female subject to male desires" (143).

The array of the protagonist's fashionable clothing and accessories surely plays a vital role in her reconquest of don Juan. Picón, in truth, dedicated solid paragraphs to Cristeta's articles of clothing, her bearing, and physical beauty to please his readers' eyes, as the title of his second chapter indicates, "En que, para satisfacción del lector, aparece una mujer bonita" (79). If, as critics claim, however, the author wanted both to entertain, and, while doing so, to contend with issues of his time that are more problematic, it is reasonable to believe that he employed the variety of the main character's fashionable outfits to achieve something more than merely to amuse his audience. In what follows, I shall demonstrate how Picón avails himself of the language of fashion to titillate his readers and, at the same time, to address the patriarchal anxieties related to the 1890s woman question in Spain, and in particular the concept of the New Woman. In addition to discussing the role of Cristeta's wardrobe in the author's vision of the *femme nouvelle*, I will show in what ways Picón's protagonist is similar to and different from the feminist views of the New Woman. I will examine how the main character's sartorial portraits in general bring to fore the writer's ambiguous (neither entirely feminist nor patriarchal) stance on changes in the ideals of femininity in late-nineteenth-century Spain.

That Cristeta's modish garments serve Picón to enthrall his readers is evident from her first appearance in the novel. Described from head to toe in lush detail, the protagonist presented herself in such splendor that it flabbergasted even an experienced seducer and a connoisseur of woman's finery, don Juan de Todellas. "El traje no podía ser más elegante. Componíanlo falda negra y plegada en menudas tablas con primoroso arte, abrigo corto de rico paño gris muy bordado … gran sombrero … y velo de tul con motas que, fingiendo lunares, sombreaba dulcemente su rostro" (81). Yet, while all the details appear to contribute equally in emphasizing the main character's exceptional beauty, the narrator seems to pay special attention to the aspects about Cristeta that most excite don Juan, among them, her feet.

One, of course, could accept the explanation that the protagonist's portrait starts with a description of her feet because, as the narrator tells us, this is the way Todellas scrutinizes every woman in his field of vision. "Don Juan miraba ... a cuantas pasaban cerca de él, y las miraba comenzando por abajo, es decir, procurando verles primero los pies ..." (80). However, given the numerous examples in the nineteenth-century narrative and culture of sexual excitement, pleasure, and thrill that a woman's feet elicit in men, it is neither accidental nor insignificant that the narrator not only commences Cristeta's picture with a description of her feet, but also makes further references to details related to them: her shoes and stockings.[1] "Los pies de la dama eran de forma irreprochable, finos, algo elevados por el tarso ... no calzados ... con medias de seda roja y zapatos de charol a la francesa, de tacón un poquito alto y sujetos con lazo de cinta negra" (80–81), asserts the narrator at the beginning of his description, only to return to similar images of Cristeta's adorned feet later in his account. "Don Juan anda ... sin poder desechar de la imaginación aquellos pies que pisan la arena como sin tocarla. Sí, el traje el mismo, menos las medias; las de ayer eran negras con lunares azules ... Martes ... en vez de zapatos, botas." (223–24). Beautiful from nature, and even more enticing when adorned in fancy shoes and stockings, Cristeta's feet *per se* do not incite her suitor's pleasure. What sends don Juan into a kind of ecstatic reverie is their status as indexical (upward pointing) objects that, according to Freud, placed in the line of vision of "the inquisitive boy [who used to peer] at the woman's genitals from below, from her legs up" (155), arouse the male with the prospect of satisfaction of his sexual desire. Although Picón published *Dulce y sabrosa* before Freud issued his study on fetishism, the novelist was able to illustrate, albeit in a humorous way, Freud's theory. He encapsulated the suitor's gaze at Cristeta's foot, and whatever else was in his upward field of vision, and arrested the sensation of delight that he experiences from glimpsing this part of her body. "Subió ella, descubriendo algo más que el pie, con lo cual don Juan quedó maravillado y suspenso, experimentando una impresión parecida a la que debió de sentir Moisés cuando le enseñaron de lejos la tierra prometida" (83).[2]

Examples of fashionable details that accentuate Cristeta's sartorial and physical beauty and, at the same time, amaze don Juan (and, with him, Picón's readers) abound in *Dulce y sabrosa*. Take, for instance, the narrator's depiction of the protagonist's veil. In bringing to focus the curiosity, uncertainty, and excitement that Cristeta's veil ignites in don Juan, Picón's narrator capitalizes on the way most nineteenth-century artists made use of this clothing item, that is, as a type of feminine adornment that produces the effects of mystery and temptation (Kessler 49–61). "La segunda vez que le sintió pasar a su lado … se oprimió el velillo contra el rostro, como queriendo recatarse, lo cual avivó en el hombre la curiosidad y la sospecha" (82), the narrator tells us. Yet, if at first the veil serves to create an aura of mystery with respect to Cristeta's identity, its role becomes more complex during the main characters' subsequent encounters. Even after don Juan manages to determine (as the beautiful passerby lifts the veil) her identity, he continues to struggle to see her face. The veil, which lures the ex-lover to catch sight of Cristeta's face while hindering his vision and to speak to her while compelling him to keep his distance ("Martes. … Ella con otro traje: falda ceniza y abrigo muy oscuro … sombrero gris con gran lazo y velillo … Don Juan, que va resuelto a hablar, se acobarda …" [224]) functions as a source of masochistic pleasure for Todellas. The more don Juan feels intrigued by it, the stronger his excitement from both the proximity to and distance from Cristeta. The deeper his uncertainty of what he believes to know and what he must guess of her present condition, the more the veil allows Picón's narrator to dramatize what Jean Baudrillard in his writings on the effects a woman's veiled face have on a man described as "the fury to unveil the truth, to get at the naked truth … [and] the impossibility of ever achieving this …" (qtd. in Kessler 54). Likewise, the scenes related to the narrator's fantasies of dressing and undressing Cristeta in her intimate apparel illustrate Picón's use of the language of fashion in depicting the protagonist's sartorial and physical beauty. The episode, for instance, in which the narrator describes don Juan imagining the main character slipping into exquisite lingerie before their rendezvous, his daydreaming about undressing her, slowly, piece by piece, as if he savors pondering every single detail of her superb garments, invites readers to share his erotic reveries.

> Su tocador, ni grande ni lujoso, respira limpieza y elegancia. Cristeta ... frente al espejo ... se quita la bata ... Las ropas interiores son finísimas; están adornadas de estrechas cintas de tonos pálidos ... Las medias son negras, como exige ... la moda; las ligas, de color de rosa. ... Ahora se pone el corsé, lleno de vistosos pespuntes, y encima ... el vestido que ... oculta el nacimiento del pecho ... ¡Qué hermosa es! ¡Cuánta cosa bonita y elegante se ha puesto! ¡Y pensar que tal vez yo se lo vaya quitando todo poco a poco ... lentamente, lazo a lazo, botón a botón, broche a broche, sin que oponga resistencia ni enfado! (260)

The strong emphasis on intimate apparel in Picón's novel should not come as a surprise, considering that the period from 1890 to 1913 was an era of extravagant consumption in women's lingerie. "Edwardian underclothes developed a degree of eroticism never previously attempted ... Never had underwear occupied so much attention in the fashion journals" observed the British fashion historian C. Willett Cunnington (*History of Underclothes* 201). Too threatening for the moral order established by the middle class that was obsessed with covering and enveloping the female body, ladies' undergarments were literally unmentionable in fashion magazines and department store catalogs until the closing decades of the nineteenth century.[3] Of course, female underclothes appealed to the erotic imagination well before the dawn of the nineteenth century. However, it was not until the 1880s that painters (Garb 115–43) and novelists, such as Zola in *Ladies Paradise* (1883), paid detailed attention to them. Light in appearance, weight, and feel "but altogether more luxurious and glamorous in conception and more exquisite and delicate in execution" (Carter 68), Edwardian lingerie was different from the utilitarian, lackluster underwear worn in the mid-Victorian period. Moreover, instead of being a subject that required silence, elegant undergarments became an essential part of a woman's *toilette*, a sign of refinement, and an indispensable component of her allure.

However, in Spain, unlike in France and the rest of Western Europe, women's underclothes remained unspeakable until almost the 1930s. Although beautiful lingerie was available to women, as Núñez Florencio observes, in "todos los tamaños, formas, y marcas" (208), it was nevertheless a taboo subject for nineteenth-century Spanish fashion magazines and conduct manuals.[4] Of course, not all writers and artists kept silent with respect to the topic of ladies' undergarments. In contrast to conservative social commentators and moralists, novelists such as Picón, and later on, Felipe Trigo, Joaquín Belda, and Eduardo Zamacois indulged their readers with descriptions of their female protagonists' intimate apparel. In providing detailed depictions of their main characters' luxurious undergarments, these writers succeeded in arresting the erotic charm of the turn-of-the-century Spanish woman (Longares 32–37; Litvak 161–72).

In *Dulce y sabrosa*, for example, the protagonist's white corset and black stockings function as a means by which Picón imaginatively conveys the concept of the *fin-de-siècle* woman as "sublime y decadente a la vez ... novia de nieve y el eros negro" (Freixa Serra 131–32) and by which he titillates his audience with images that he opted not to express explicitly. "The proper and virtuous woman ... wears a white satin corset; never a colored corset," an anonymous author wrote in 1881 in *La Vie Parisienne* (qtd. in Steele, *The Corset* 117). In drawing attention to the white color and plain design of Cristeta's corset as well as to don Juan's dreams of her (even after she had already been seduced) as "la florecilla humilde ... sencillísima, blanca" (202), the narrator reinforces the image of the main character as a *novia de nieve*: modest, delicate, and pure. In contrast, the black stockings confer upon Cristeta's body an aura of lingering sensuality. Associated throughout the nineteenth century with female lust and perversity (Steele, *Fetish* 132), the black stockings (in which Cristeta always appears tantalizingly close yet unreachable to her lover) bring forward the narrator's fantasy of her as an *eros negro*. Unobtainable, and, at the same time, erotically alluring, she epitomizes the image, which, as Bram Dijkstra has shown, was pervasive in the end-of-the-century imagination: a virgin and a carnal temptress (383–85). "Llevaba falda ... corta para lucir los pies, calzados con medias negras y zapatitos a la francesa ... él ... llamándola en voz baja: —¡Cristeta, Cristeta mía! ... Ella ... indiferente y desdeñosa ... —No, Juan, tuya no" (249–50).

In addition to employing details of Cristeta's lingerie to stir up "a mix of innocence and sensuality" ("Introduction," *Sweet and Delectable* 24), as Valis put it, the narrator uses them to create images that he does not express plainly. Consider once more the symbolic meaning of the protagonist's simple white corset at the beginning of her first lovemaking with don Juan: "La mano izquierda de don Juan se posó sobre la doble y turgente redondez del pecho de Cristeta ... Poco después, el corsé ... caía sobre la alfombrilla al pie del sofá ... Pero, ¡tente pluma!" (163). By emphasizing the act of Cristeta's undressing rather than her undressed body, the narrator titillates his readers by promising, delaying, and ultimately leaving to their imagination the bedroom scene's denouement. More importantly, he avails himself of the corset as the most expressive vehicle for Cristeta's nakedness.

The idea of deploying sexually charged articles of clothing to create images of a female nude was certainly not novel at the dawn of the nineteenth century. According to fashion historian Anne Hollander, for most artists throughout the centuries, the cloth and the flesh, rather than the flesh alone, provided a powerful expression of female nudity. Tintoretto in his *Susannah and the Elders*, for instance, brings the main character's corset to the foreground to capture the immediacy of Susannah's naked beauty. "The erotic message has been shifted to the surrounding emblems; the nude figure itself does not have to convey it," wrote Hollander with reference to Tintoretto's painting (*Seeing through Clothes* 161). "Susannah's body has been more eroticized by her abandoned corset than by any of its extraordinary linear distortions" (Hollander, *Seeing through Clothes* 161). Similarly in Picón's scene, the corset falling slowly (as the narrator's choice of the verb *caía*, instead of *cayó*, indicates) beside Cristeta's sofa produces a far more intense image of her nudity than any references to her breasts or any other part of her bare flesh.

While images of Cristeta's sartorial and physical beauty are implemented in *Dulce y sabrosa* to provide readers with pleasure, the same clothing items and bodily features that the author uses to create these images serve him to address an issue that was the subject of ongoing debate at the time he published his novel, namely, "the woman question." It is true that Picón, unlike his contemporaries, did not pen a single essay on feminism. In fact, the novelist's position on "the woman question" remains, as critics have often pointed out, far from straightforward (Gold 65–68; Mandrell 171; Landry 137). Yet, "the consistency with which Picón undertakes ... on the man/woman relationship ... and the variations with which he tempers this ... theme" (Sobejano, "Introduction," *Moral Divorce* 19) in his narrative, show that the author of *Dulce y sabrosa* did not refrain from articulating, albeit indirectly, his views on the feminists' demands for equal opportunity in education and

Chapter Five

professional development. They also demonstrate that Picón did not shy away from responding to patriarchal anxieties related to the emerging concept of the New Woman and her quest for freedom in sexuality and marriage.

How do Picón's portrayals of Cristeta in her exquisite lingerie, with a veil covering her face, and elegantly adorned legs and feet contradict the Spanish conservative writers', moralists', and social commentators' vision of the New Woman? It is worth mentioning that even though it was first in 1894 that the English press used the term the "New Woman," her image—recurrently conveyed in the vocabulary of the grotesque—had already haunted the conservative male writers' and journalists' imagination in the late 1880s and early 1890s. A figure of mannish appearance "[i]n France, the *femme nouvelle* was often caricatured as a *cerveline*," wrote Elaine Showalter, "a dried-up pedant with an oversized head; an androgynous flat-chested *garçonnet*, more like a teenage boy than a woman; or a masculine *hommesse*" (39). Similarly in Spain—the New Woman portrayed as a gender rebel, "who assumed the right to live, dress, and act in defiance of bourgeois norms of feminine behaviour" (Jagoe, *Ambiguous Angels* 156)—was lampooned in Spanish narrative, drawings, and press.[5] However, as one can see in Picón's *Dulce y sabrosa*, not all male writers projected their vision of the New Woman in this manner. If Cristeta, because of her active pursuit of a career as an actress, her inner strength, and steadfast wish for personal sovereignty, fits the profile of the *femme nouvelle*, Picón's portrayals of her physical and sartorial beauty clearly contradict the way his conservative colleagues described the external appearance of the New Woman.[6] Consider again the scenes dedicated to the nuances of the main character's intimate apparel. According to the British fashion historian Caroline Cox, "[t]he first items of seductive lingerie were worn by the New Women of the 1890s ... to offset the 'mannish' accusations directed at [her]" (130–32). Thus, it is hardly a coincidence that Picón's narrator emphasizes Cristeta's feminine qualities such as her corporal beauty, her sensuality, and charm, not only through the richness of her sartorial creations, but also through the elaborate depictions of her underwear. Likewise, the narrator's attention to the protagonist's veil relates to Picón's position on patriarchal fears of feminine sexuality and the apocalyptic images of the New Woman. Described as an evil temptress, monstrous, perverse, and destructive, the figure of the veiled female had much in common with the New Woman who also often was portrayed as either sexually devouring (incapable of love) or rejecting others' affection (Dijkstra 215–16, 265). Significantly, as the veiled woman and the *femme nouvelle* incarnated the terra incognita in terms of their sexuality and were both considered a threat to the sexual status quo in that they undermined the conventional conception of gender relations (i.e., challenged male supremacy), they both engendered intense hostility and fright among conservative men.

Picón's efforts to downplay the threat of feminine sexual power are evident in the references to Cristeta's veil. Even though the act of Cristeta's unveiling produces disquiet in don Juan ("en todas partes creyó tenerla delante de los ojos. Unos momentos le miraba cariñosa, otros le sonreía burlona" [84]), the narrator's use of the diminutive form of the veil as well as the description of the main character's beautiful features behind it neutralize, if not denounce, the absurdity of the male fears of the allegedly perilous veiled/unveiled Medusa/Salome female figure.

> En el instante de arrancar el carruaje, la desconocida se alzó el velillo. Don Juan pudo dudar mientras vio el rostro al través del tul; pero toda perplejidad quedó desvanecida al mirarlo libre de aquel adorno. ¡Qué cara! Los ojos eran azules, oscuros, hermosísimos; la boca un poquito grande ... las facciones delicadas; las orejas chicas; la expresión de la fisonomía entre seria y picaresca. (83–84)

Similar to the feminist representation of *Salome* by the American artist Ella Ferris Pell, which was exhibited in Paris in 1890, a year before Picón published *Dulce y sabrosa*, the author's depiction of Cristeta with her veil raised diverges strongly from his male colleagues', writers', and painters' versions of an unveiled threatening female figure (Showalter 145–61). Like Pell's *Salome*, Picón's unveiled Cristeta is beautiful, healthy, vigorous, independent, and young. Moreover, liberated from the veil, Picón's protagonist does not gaze, as Dijkstra wrote about Pell's *Salome*, "with a look of crazed sexual hunger ... does not have the wan, vampire features of the serpentine dancer ... Instead, she is a woman of flesh and blood" (392). She is not only capable of giving and receiving affection but also still very much in love with don Juan.

There is no doubt that Cristeta's act of unveiling her face produces anxiety in her ex-lover. Yet, the uneasiness that don Juan experiences as the lovely lady lifts her veil has less to do with her sexual power and more with his own uncertainty of how to interpret her appearance. "Se había perdido ya de vista el coche, y don Juan seguía inmóvil pensando: Esto es increíble. ¿Estará *con alguno*? … ¿Se habrá casado?" (83–84; Picón's italics). What causes Picón's character sleepless nights are his hesitation mixed with anxiety, analogous to fears provoked by the *femme nouvelle* among nineteenth-century intellectuals and conservative men. Like don Juan, these men did not know what to make of the New Woman's conduct, her assertiveness, and independence. They were clueless where to place her in society, and, most of all, how to deal with her. Similar to Cristeta, this type of woman did not fall into any category of lady who men like don Juan were accustomed to handling, at least, until now. "¿Por dónde iba a comenzar? ¿Qué táctica seguiría? … ¿qué iba a solicitar?" (248). "¿Qué mujer es ésta? —se decía al entrar en su casa— ¿La coqueta más temible del mundo, o una desdichada que fluctúa entre el deber y el amor?" (301).

Significantly, it is not a coincidence that after the unveiling, Picón dedicates long paragraphs not to Cristeta's inner thoughts—but to don Juan's—in which the ex-lover recalls details of his affair with her, analyzes his present feelings, and ponders his future prospects. If a woman's gesture of raising her veil engenders anxiety in a male, it is because, as Sandra M. Gilbert and Susan Gubar assert in *The Madwoman in the Attic*, this particular item of the feminine wardrobe suggests for him the possibility to access another sphere, another sexuality, another self. In other words, this gesture is frightening to a character like Picón's don Juan, because to penetrate the female veil does not necessarily mean to unravel the mystery of feminine sexuality. It also bears the possibility of leading to an act of self-revelation for men.

Moreover, the references to Cristeta's feet have much to do with the author's position on the patriarchal fears related to feminists' demands for women's sexual liberation. As mentioned before, it is hardly accidental that the protagonist's portrait and the descriptions of the other women in El Retiro begin with a depiction of their feet. Writing about fashion in Europe in general, Lola Gavarrón affirmed that "hasta 1914, la mujer no mostrará públicamente sus tobillos" (29). In Spain, according to Adolfo Perinat and María Isabel Marrades, "las piernas emergen … en el campo visual al capricho de la moda de los años veinte" (136), and even then "fugaces se aperciben sus líneas al subir al tranvía o al carruaje" (Perinat and Marrades 136). Thus, the scenes of Cristeta displaying her foot while getting into a carriage in El Retiro as well as allowing don Juan to look at her shoes and stockings during subsequent strolls carry the author's critique of restrictive sexual mores. Through them, Picón legitimized an alternative notion of gender and desire. By presenting scenes in which Cristeta exhibits her feet as natural and by referring to her shoes and stockings as aspects that add to her womanly charm, Picón clearly did not endorse the false modesty that for centuries obligated "las damas españolas, orgullosas como nadie de sus finos piececitos … [tener] vedado el enseñarlos a quien quiera que fuese del sexo opuesto" (Gavarrón 121). Certainly, in the moments when the protagonist makes a display of her feet, she breaks with the traditional notion of a woman as a passive object of male admiration in that she usurps the power of the gaze by manipulating it to her advantage. However, even so, she is still far from incarnating the seductive, sexually liberated *femme fatal* who haunted men's imagination as an individual preying on male flesh. It is true that in seizing agency and maneuvering don Juan's attention to her physical and sartorial beauty (i.e., her feet and their adornment), Cristeta wins the prize and reconquers her ex-lover's affection. However, while she temporarily exploits her position as an object of beauty (in that she entices the man to look at her feet), her actions are not motivated by revenge on don Juan or ambition to reverse the traditional gender roles. Instead, her behavior is governed by her wish to gratify her own desire: "Mucho he sufrido, pero todo lo doy por bien empleado, porque al verte seguirme, y perseguirme … he llegado a creer que me amas de veras" (347).

Picón's criticism of the patriarchal stance on "the woman question" certainly does not mean that the author had no reservations about feminists' demands related to the issue. As the account of Cristeta's career as an actress indicates, Picón was skeptical of the viability of feminists' claims for economic independence and the quality of opportunities available for women to participate in the public workplace. "Women who operated within the public sphere were analogous to prostitutes, the original 'working girls'" (*Cigar Smoke* 58), explains Joyce Tolliver with respect to the nineteenth-century cultural context within which women who

Chapter Five

attempted to join the "legitimate" labor force were viewed by *fin-de-siècle* Spanish society and the press. "With the exception of the nun, the schoolteacher, and possibly the queen, any woman who located her work outside the home," affirmed Tolliver, "was by definition of questionable morality and thus fair game for sexual exploitation" (*Cigar Smoke* 58). Such is the case of actresses and chorus girls working in the theater in *Dulce y sabrosa*. Although the narrator takes pains to point out that Cristeta, unlike her female colleagues, does not compromise her virtue for the sake of money or sartorial gifts, the theater is a place of erotic commerce where women's bodies are reduced to the status of commodities for sale.[7]

> El público ... se componía casi exclusivamente de hombres aficionados a comprar hecho el amor, y de pecadoras elegantes. A última hora se ponían las piezas y zarzuelitas más verdes, y cual si esto les sirviese de aperitivo, era de ver cómo a la salida muchos caballeros, o vestidos de tales, esperaban en la calle la salida de bailarinas, coristas y figurantas ... cada hombre se llevaba su prójima ... y ya formadas las parejas ... todos se iban contentos; ellas haciéndose las conquistadas, y ellos imaginando triunfo lo que, a lo más, era compra. (96)

In juxtaposing Cristeta's earlier dreams of the theater as a temple to beauty and art to the crude reality that nightlife entertainment represents, Picón criticized feminists' naïveté in glamorizing the idea of women joining the workforce in the public sphere without considering the consequences that these women would have to pay for doing so. "El teatro y el arte que ella se había fingido leyendo dramas y comedias en la trastienda del estanco ... no eran el arte y el teatro que la realidad le presentaba. Soñó con una vida toda poesía y encanto, y tropezó con una existencia llena de vulgaridad y desilusión" (126). Overall, the narrative voice does not hide that Cristeta's popularity as an actress depends entirely on the way she looks in her costumes or rather the scarcity of clothing items she wears in front of her audience. As the narrator's descriptions of her older female colleagues' poverty, greed, and prostitution (as exemplified by Carola) imply, the theater provides women with neither the opportunity for serious professional development nor the chance to gain economic independence from men. "Era aplaudida por elegante, picaresca, graciosa y bonita, o por salir medio desnuda ... rara vez la celebraban como artista" (126).[8] Nonetheless, where Picón concurred with feminists' ideas on "the woman question," was in his views on moral issues. If the author was not, as Sobejano put it, "un feminista si por feminismo se entiende el programa social de igualación de los derechos de la mujer a los del hombre en todos los terrenos y principalmente en el económico (o laboral) y en el político ..." ("Introducción," *Dulce y sabrosa* 27), he surely supported women's right to free themselves from concepts such as virginity, prostitution, and adultery that "reduce them to the status of an object that is weakened, worn down and ruined" ("Introduction," *Moral Divorce* 20). Although Picón was quick to emphasize that don Juan is the first and only man in Cristeta's life, her ways of remembering her intimate moments with her lover—taking pleasure in recalling the sound of the corset and the rest of her clothing falling down—show that she neither regrets nor feels ashamed or embarrassed by them.

> ¡La deshonra! ¿Qué le importaba? ¿Ni a qué echar de menos el encanto de la doncellez si jamás había de sentir no poder ofrecérselo a otro hombre? ... Las escenas ... que Cristeta se complacía en evocar ... eran reminiscencias espontáneas ... el ruido rápido que producen las trencillas del corsé al deslizarse por entre los ojetes metálicos; luego caían sobre la alfombra las ropas ... no todo lo que Cristeta sentía era deliciosamente impuro ... Sí; cien cuerpos quisiera tener para que él ... los poseyera, y cada noche una virginidad para entregársela. (198–99)

In addition, the last scene in the novel, in which Cristeta chooses free union over marriage, reinforces the notion that "las narraciones de Jacinto Octavio Picón ... adelantan el tipo de mujer moderna mucho antes de que se hiciera real" (Miguel 164). After all, none of the protagonists labeled by critics as the New Woman in the late-nineteenth-century Spanish narrative, such as Tristana Reluz in Galdós's *Tristana* (1892) or Feíta Neira in Pardo Bazán's *Memorias de un solterón* (1896), renounced matrimony in favor of free union. However, one should not be too hasty in considering Cristeta an embodiment of "el arquetipo femenino ... nada tradicional y sí moderno" (Valdés Sánchez 347). As Amando de Miguel explained, "la mujer que 'pierde su honra' con un hombre a lo más que puede aspirar es a casarse con él ... En la práctica sólo se abre la vía de la prostitución ... La solución de la boda forzada con el burlador (ya lo dice la palabra) se presta a chanzas y menosprecios" (156). Had Cristeta opted for free union without losing her virginity to don Juan, she would be the full-fledged modern woman that, in Ivón Valdés Sánchez's words, "se diferencia de la tradicional en la libre capacidad de elegir su vida, y en el modo y la manera de vivirla" (353). Given, however, "la famosa dualidad entre mujeres honradas y perdidas" (Miguel 165) in nineteenth-century bourgeois society and Cristeta's "pertenencia a la categoría residual de 'las otras'" (Miguel 164), her decision not to tie the nuptial knot with Todellas remains much more within the parameters of the conventional gender order than it might first appear.

Of course, to bring to the surface the protagonist's sexual experience as a natural part of her development as a woman and to allow her to speak in favor of free union was, no doubt, a bold undertaking on Picón's part.[9] For even the thought that the leading characters could be happier as *pareja de hecho* than as a married couple—especially "en una sociedad como la española finisecular, cuyo interés principal," affirmed Hazel Gold, "reside en alinear en cuanto posible las leyes de la pasión con las leyes de propiedad privada y de reproducción" (70)—entails a threat to bourgeois sexual mores. Yet, as much as Picón "se adelanta a su tiempo en la formulación de sus problemas en la sociedad en la que vive ... no está dispuesto a transigir con los modelos culturales dominantes" (Valdés Sánchez 348). In fact, as numerous juxtapositions of up-to-date and traditional sartorial images of Cristeta attest, the novelist inserted various traits of a conventional woman in the portrait of the protagonist. Consider once more the scene in El Retiro in which Picón's narrator introduces the main character to the reader. Immediately after describing Cristeta in her modish outfit, the narrator includes don Juan's own private vision of how she would look as an exquisitely dressed, conventional bourgeois woman, either waiting or resting after the ball. Here, the suitor clearly delights in imagining her "envuelta en una bata lujosa, lánguidamente tumbada en una butaca, o vestida de baile con los brazos desnudos, ceñido el cuerpo en sedas y encajes ..." (81).[10] Similarly, during the first meeting of the young actress and don Juan in the theater, the narrator juxtaposes the description of Cristeta in a flashy common gypsy costume with the idealized vision of her: "con un traje de baile, de raso muy claro ... y con un gran abrigo forrado de pieles que le llegase hasta los pies ... Nada de alhajas ..." (107). Finally, there are episodes in the novel where Picón's narrator resorts to sartorial images to underscore the protagonist's bourgeois virtues of thrift, hard work, and loyalty.

> Su vida fue desde entonces toda recogimiento y prudencia. Por la mañana temprano se alisaba el pelo, sin tufos, rizos, ni flequillo; se vestía modestamente, y comenzaba a despachar en el estanco sin más descanso que el preciso para almorzar y comer. Luego de cerrada la tienda, se retiraba a su cuarto y allí poblada de recuerdos su triste soledad, o lloraba, doliéndole como a verdadera enamorada, antes la injusticia del abandono, que la crueldad de la deshonra. (198)

There is certainly more than one reason for which Picón's sartorial portraits of Cristeta allude to "the woman question" and in particular to the concept of the New Woman, but, at the same time, these portraits resist easy identification with either feminist or patriarchal views on this matter. As the author's supportive attitude toward moral issues indicates and his skepticism toward feminists' claims for economic independence and professional opportunities shows, it is reasonable to believe that while he was in general sympathetic with feminists' ideas to improve conditions for women in Spain, he was not in agreement with all of their pursuits and demands. In addition, considering the fact that Picón wrote during a time marked by hostile reaction among conservative intellectuals toward "the woman question," it would make sense that he did not have much faith in Spanish society's readiness to accept new modes of feminine conduct based on women's quests for financial and sexual autonomy. It is unsurprising, therefore, that he was cautious in expressing his support of the women's cause. As Gold affirmed with regard to Picón's eluding descriptions of lovemaking scenes in *Dulce y sabrosa*, "el autor implícito, dejando ver su propia filiación de clase media, se ve imposibilitado de articular verbalmente una conducta sexual que, además de considerarse tabú para las sensibilidades de muchos lectores españoles, también serviría de arma de destrucción del sistema entero en que se apoyaba la hegemonía burguesa" (74). Finally, the insistence on Picón's part on the purpose of the novel to entertain the reader lends itself to suggestion that perhaps the author considered it counterproductive to try too hard to convince the conservative sector to come to terms with changes with respect to "the woman question." These changes already were occurring everywhere else in the Western world and were undoubtedly on their way to Spain (Jagoe, *Ambiguous Angels* 120–55).

Nevertheless, despite his ambiguous stance on the issue, Picón created an uncommon image of the New Woman in *Dulce y sabrosa*. According to Lou Charnon-Deutsch, one can distinguish between two types of the New Woman in the nineteenth-century Spanish narrative. The first kind longed for increased educational and professional opportunity and challenged patriarchy for rights unjustly denied to her to make decisions regarding her body. The second kind refused to play the role of primping doll and insisted on being a working, contributing member of society (*Narratives of Desire* 144–45). Picón's Cristeta fits both categories. As we have seen, she makes up her own mind with respect to her body and rarely leans on others for financial support throughout the novel. Yet what grants the main character equally, if not more, the status of the beyond-the-norm *femme nouvelle* is her ability to recognize her options as a working-class woman within her society at that time. Of course, her decision to continue her relationship in free union could be seen as disappointing in that, as James Mandrell wrote, "Don Juan gets everything that he wants and needs, including his freedom and the passion of love" (189). At the same time, it is not entirely true that Cristeta, by becoming "like a wife, virtuous and submissive" (Mandrell 189), gives up being the strong independent woman that readers had known until now. Picón's narrator cleverly conveys this message through the language of clothing in the last scene. In it, Cristeta tosses her superb wardrobe of a wealthy, married woman on the bed and replaces it with modest, plain garments in which she appears before don Juan. In this way, the narrator shows that in renouncing marriage for freedom and love the protagonist remains the same: assertive, independent, and brave. She acknowledges and accepts that caring for don Juan is the only rewarding option open to her. "Yo te serviré en el bien, de estímulo, en el mal, de rémora. Duplicaré tus venturas y compartiré tus penas … tú, libre como el aire; yo esclava, quieta, callada y mansa …" (348–49). Furthermore, she is confident and capable of growing into the realization that she will be able to retain more control over her personal life and over her relationship with don Juan as an ideal mate to him than if she were to marry him: "Vive tranquilo. Si he hecho tanto para que vuelvas a mí, ¿qué no seré capaz de hacer por merecerte y conservarte?" (349). The final thoughts of don Juan ("Será mi mujer" [349]) aptly capture the incomprehensibility of a bourgeois man (and of the society in general) toward the New Woman's unconventional way of thinking: "Si me caso le pierdo" (349). Cristeta's decision is, in a way, similar to the choice that Pardo Bazán's Feíta Neira will make some years later in the sense that both women attempt to encounter freedom in a companionship with a man. Her choice, moreover, like Feíta's, does not rest "upon any innate craving for dependency but on her growing awareness of what social realities are open to her … her evolving maturity that permits her to take advantage of the limited resources available to her …" (Charnon-Deutsch, *Narratives of Desire* 173–74).

There is no doubt that Picón paid a steep price for his portrait of the New Woman. His protagonist's final decision was too radical for the conservative sector, since it questioned the value of marriage. Conversely, it was not radical enough or, perhaps, simply too utopian for the liberal audience. Therefore, it is not surprising that *Dulce y sabrosa* received (and still does) scarce attention from readers and critics alike (Valis, *The Novels of Picón* 142–43; Valdés Sánchez 343–44). Still, Picón achieved something important in his work. By entertaining his audience—as he promised at the outset of his novel—with the variety of Cristeta's sartorial creations, the author cajoled his readers to envision a rather positive image of the New Woman. At the same time, by using the language of fashion and by depicting his protagonist dressed at times in her breath-taking modish garments and, at times, in a conservative modest wardrobe, he managed to convey, in an elegant way, the tension and anxieties surrounding the new ideals of femininity in late-nineteenth-century Spain.

Conclusion

A close examination of the stylish characters' portrayals in Galdós's, Pardo Bazán's, and Picón's narratives shows that the art of dressing offered a solid platform from which late-nineteenth-century writers explored cultural and social forces that shaped modern life in Spain. As a cultural phenomenon, fashion was entrenched as much in the disruption of the visible social hierarchies of the Ancien Regime, the process of urbanization, and the development of modern consumerism, as in the destabilization of traditional gender roles. As such, it provided an exceptionally fertile ground for revision—albeit from different perspectives, as one can see from the analysis of the above-mentioned authors' works—of the dominant ideals of femininity and masculinity in Spain. Urban spectacle, economic activity, and the superficial notion of progress are the significant features in Galdós's portrait of Isidora Rufete in *La desheredada* and his depiction of the would-be dandy Manuel Pez in *La de Bringas*. Sexual and social mores are at the heart of Pardo Bazán's description of Asís Taboada and Diego Pacheco in *Insolación* where details of the elegant couple's outward appearances are implicated in the author's veiled critique of the rules of conduct and courtship assigned by society to each gender. In addition, the aesthetic formation of the New Woman—clad in a variety of theatrical costumes and sexy lingerie to mark her pursuit of economic and sexual freedom, but feminine enough in her manner of dress not to pose a serious threat to the prevailing notions of womanhood—is the central aspect of Picón's vision of the modern woman. The varied stances and, consequently, the emphasis on the diverse points of convergence between fashion and modernity in these novelists' representations of one aspect of modern life—gender—make it apparent that as readers we should approach the richness of the voguish details from more than one angle. In particular, it is worth looking beyond perspectives from which we have interpreted them already: class distinction and/or female vanity.

I wish to underline that the argument of this book is not at all to contend that fashion is not about one's social aspiration and/or reflection of one's self-love. "Of course dress does 'speak' status" (*Adorned in Dreams* 9), as Elizabeth Wilson put it clearly. After all, every character who is in tune with the latest style in Galdós's, Pardo Bazán's, and Picón's novels dresses to mark his or her position (whether real or desired) in society. However, in the age of mass production, clothing—once a signifier of class, rank, and occupation—can hardly be considered a reliable source to establish one's social position. In fact, as the countless observations of the conservative and progressive intellectuals already before and during the nineteenth century indicated (in Spain and the rest of the Western world) and as summarized by Anne Hollander, "dressing to make ambiguous one's exact identity is a very common game" (*Seeing through Clothes* 347). Additionally, in the case of nineteenth-century Spain there is a disparity, as Noël Valis indicated, "between the perception of middleclassness and the economic, material conditions required to produce it" (*The Culture* 11). As Valis explained further, "the adoption of certain life styles and attitudes can and [does] exist even when the economic structure lags behind, that is, when there is a perception of being modern despite insufficient modernization" (*The Culture* 11). So, as one can see from the stylish characters' portraits in the novels under discussion, dressing smartly in order to be modern (if at times merely on the surface) turns out to be as powerful a drive behind these protagonists' pursuit of fashion as their desire to distinguish themselves through their voguish outfits from lower orders of society.

Of course, to discuss fashion in connection with gender and in the context of Spain's transition to modernity is also only one way to interpret the modish characters' elaborate *toilettes* in the aforementioned literary texts. My examination of the significance of their sartorial portraits is then obviously only partial and, hence, open-ended. At the same time, however, the analysis of the interrelation between fashion, gender, and modernity provides new insights into commonly accepted bourgeois notions of womanhood and manhood in late-nineteenth-century Spain. The attention in this book to the male interest in dressing stylishly, for example, challenges the prevailing cliché that fashion was exclusively a woman's domain in nineteenth-century Spain. The discussion of the ways in which the seemingly insignificant details in men's attire contributed to bringing to light the inconsistencies in the allegedly stable cultural construction of nineteenth-century masculinity in Galdós's and Pardo Bazán's works points further to the sartorial art as a crucial visual device in doña Emilia's efforts to reformulate the traditional masculine role. In other words, the supposedly unchanging rules of the male art of dressing proved invaluable as a means for Pardo Bazán to expose the fissures and contradictions in the normative notions of bourgeois manhood in the late 1880s. They provided her with a medium to convey that amendments to the conventional norms of manhood constituted the necessary condition for changes in gender relations and, in particular, woman's position in the society. Through the link between fashion and masculinity, in sum, Pardo Bazán was able to express that the reconfigurations of traditional gender constructs (womanhood *and* manhood) were the vital steps in Spain's process of modernization.

That in the modern age the art of dressing "is ... implicated more fully in the representation of gender, and particularly in the management of tensions between the masculine and the feminine" (Finkelstein 57), than the struggle for social prestige and private vice is well illustrated in the works of the next generations of Spanish writers.[1] Ramón del Valle-Inclán's deployed finery in his descriptions of Brandomín's fetishistic fascination with Concha (Litvak 119, 122–23) and the inversion of sexual gender roles in *Sonata de otoño* (1902). For Felipe Trigo, depictions in minute detail of his leading ladies' provocative outfits and intimate apparel in *Las ingenuas* (1901) and other novels (Litvak 162–69) constituted an effective means for his powerful representations of female sexuality. Thus, as these examples indicate, writers of the early-twentieth-century availed themselves readily of fashionable features to explore the shifting state of man-woman relations and the new types of femininity and masculinity in Spain.[2]

Significant in this context is the *modus operandi* in which novelists such as Trigo used the language of fashion (particularly with respect to the prevailing attitudes to sex and feminine sexuality) to contest and rearticulate the dominant gender norms. As the content and form of Trigo's works evince, there could be little doubt that nineteenth-century authors paved the way for the next generation of writers for engaging the sartorial signs to address gender issues of their time in more daring and direct ways. Consider, for instance, Trigo's credo that a change in a woman's socioeconomic position (and in gender relations in general) "deberá ser paralela a la revolución erótica" (Litvak 213), as only then, "la mujer perderá falsos pudores y se adentrará ... para gozar de todas las posibilidades del cuerpo y de la carne como deberá gozar de las de la mente" (213). Trigo's position resembles Picón's endorsement—via sartorial luxuries—of relaxations of sexual norms and women's liberation from such concepts as false modesty, virginity, and marriage in *Dulce y sabrosa*. It is hardly a coincidence, moreover, that the author of *Las ingenuas* opted to give voice to his stance in a similar way as Picón, namely, as Litvak demonstrated, through an abundance of modish subtleties.

Yet, it is the nature of Galdós's, Pardo Bazán's, and Picón's aesthetic reactions (i.e., the manners in which they applied their vast knowledge of *la moda*), rather than the solutions that they provided in response to the shifting limits of both genders, that I have sought to highlight in my examination of the function of fashion in these authors' works. As one can see from the analysis of their texts, solutions are not always offered—purposely so, in the case in Galdós's portrayal of Manuel Pez in *La de Bringas* and Isidora Rufete in *La desheredada*. Instead, the position of these novelists (sometimes because of their own gender, as with Pardo Bazán) is highly ambivalent. However, it is precisely the ambiguity, stemming from the ability of fashion to reinforce and to subvert the established order (not only with respect to gender, but also to sexuality, class, and other aspects of life) and, concurrently, the power to express one's creativity, imagination, and inner desires that are of interest here. They explain, in my view, Galdós's, Pardo Bazán's, and Picón's persistent reliance on the sartorial muse to depict the shift (or at times only a superficial attempt to move from the traditional to modern notions of womanhood and manhood) and to deal, in general, with a matter as complex and controversial as the gender concerns of their time.

As I hope to have demonstrated in this study, fashion is not a phenomenon that one can reduce to the realm of material objects or explain without impoverishing its meaning in the works of each of the authors under discussion only from socio-economic and/or moral standpoints. Instead, its multidimensional and contradictory manifestations in the nineteenth-century Spanish novel bear connection with an array of issues. These issues include national and cultural identity, the crises of traditional values and anxiety over the loss of imperial power, the invasion of foreign (e.g., French) vocabulary and fashion terminology, popular culture, to name only a few areas of study that have been to some extent addressed, but still await further exploration. Related to this observation is Jesus Cruz's emphasis on the importance and scarcity (in the field of history) of studies dedicated to everyday experiences and the social and cultural customs of the rising middle class in nineteenth-century Spain. In his recent examination of bourgeois culture and modernity, the historian claimed, "Spanish nineteenth-century middle classes have been mainly studied for their politics and their structural weaknesses rather than their cultural habits" (Cruz 5). Fortunately, wrote Cruz, "recent research from the perspective of cultural studies, literary analysis, and visual culture provides new understandings of the nature of Spanish modernity by considering the Spanish case in its specific historical context and in its diversity of manifestations" (5). As my references to recent scholarship on the cultural formation and development of the nineteenth-century Spanish middle class indicate, the link between fashion and gender, modernity and gender, fashion and modernity, and, at times, among all three of these phenomena, did not escape critics' attention. In this respect, my investigation inserts itself within the studies that address the lifestyle, cultural values, and aesthetic inclinations of the nineteenth-century Spanish bourgeoisie in connection to Spain's project of modernization. By focusing exclusively on the manners in which the aforementioned novelists deployed their protagonists' fashionable *toilettes* to question and reformulate the dominant gender norms, the objective of this work was to provide contemporary readers with a broader perspective on ways in which Spanish bourgeois women and men negotiated their places in society and on these authors' positions on Spain's integration into modernity.

Yet, the sartorial art is a complex phenomenon. Given that dressing chic is not about clothing *per se* but rather about the style in which one carries oneself in it and in doing so, marks one's relation to one's gendered body (Entwistle and Wilson 6–8),

Conclusion

one could infer much more from the multilayered significance of fashionable female and male bodies. The ongoing research on the intersections between fashion, gender, and modernity and on the ways in which the dressed body is part of one's living experience, an intonation, a specific way of being a woman and a man in the modern world (Entwistle and Wilson; Moi) promises a fruitful ground for further explorations. In this sense, my work is an invitation for both a revision of the commonly accepted, oversimplified meaning of the everyday experience—dressing *à la mode*—in Galdós's, Pardo Bazán's, and Picón's novels and for further investigations of the role that fashion played in reformulation of dominant gender norms as a part of Spain's project of modernization.

Notes

Introduction

1. I refer to modernity as both the term that applies to the process of industrialization and urbanization of Spain, as well as, in Rita Felski's words, "the more general experience of the aestheticization of everyday life, as exemplified in the ephemeral and transitory qualities of an urban culture shaped by the imperatives of fashion, consumerism, and constant innovation" (13).

2. These are, of course, merely examples of recent studies in which scholars paid attention to the importance of fashion.

3. Thorstein Veblen's theory is the one most relied on by scholars of the nineteenth-century Spanish narrative. For examples of its recent application in the context of Spanish literature and culture, see Anderson 54–55 and McKinney 49–50.

4. For the importance of clothing in the characterization of Spanish society in *Tormento*, consult Wright.

5. In her study on the importance of fashion in literature from 1728 to 1926, Ana María Díaz Marcos devoted one chapter to the in-depth analysis of one Restoration narrative: *La de Bringas* (1884). In her chapter, in contrast to my study of this novel, which centers in chapter 2 exclusively on the male character Manuel Pez, Díaz Marcos (while paying some attention to the smartly dressed politician) examined in detail the luxury-obsessed female protagonist: Rosalía Bringas.

6. Similarly, Cadalso en *Cartas marruecas* (1793) described the male attraction to fashion and luxuries as follows: "El poderoso de este siglo … ¿en qué gasta sus rentas? Despiértanle dos ayudas de cámara primorosamente peinados y vestidos … pónese una camisa finísima de Holanda, luego una bata de mucho gusto tejida en León de Francia … viste a la dirección de un sastre y peluquero francés … y, al tiempo de acostarse, puede decir … Doy gracias al cielo de que todas mis operaciones de hoy han sido dirigidas a echar fuera de mi patria cuanto oro y plata ha estado en mi poder" (143–44). On the association between eighteenth-century women's passion for sartorial luxury, moral depravity, and idleness, see Aldaraca, *El Ángel del Hogar* 96–102 and Haidt, *Women, Work, and Clothing* 66–81. On the figure of the eighteenth-century man of fashion, consult Haidt, *Embodying Enlightenment* 111–50 and Díaz Marcos 49–101.

7. Rodríguez-Solís's portraits of Spanish women from the period 1800–24 attested to the lack of modesty in their dressing style. "No todas usaban trajes oscuros sino ricas mantillas blancas de encajes; fastuosa peineta; vestidos de raso azul y carmesí con encajes, bolillas y alamares y rica pasamanería; con elegantes y coquetones zapatos de respingada punta: o trajes blancos ligeros y ceñidos de los llamados *volubilís*; peinado de estilo griego y llamativa banda de rosas al pecho" (102; Rodríguez-Solís's italics). According to this author, Spanish men were attired just as elegantly as the ladies of the time. "Lucía chupa blanca bordada en colores a realce; chorrera de siete listones de encaje de Bruselas; corbatín blanco; calzón de punto; casaca de piqué de seda ... sombrero apuntado, siempre bajo del brazo para no estropear el peinado ... y para el interior de casa la elegante bata de *filipichí*" (103; Rodríguez-Solís's italics).

8. Decades later, also Antonio Flores's accounts of changes in the retail system and the effects of new marketing techniques and the abundance of fashionable goods on potential customers, attested to further development of the commercial world in Madrid. In the article "Los escaparates," from his collection of essays *La sociedad de 1850*, Flores observed: "De escaparate en escaparate, como quien camina por un inmenso túnel de cristal, pasaremos una y otra calle ... cuantos objetos de lujo ha podido inventar la coquetería de la industria para engañar y seducir al oro. ... Detrás del escaparate hay una dama ... que a medida que va empañando con su aliento el cristal que se interpone entre su belleza y el aderezo de perlas, se vaya empañando su virtud ... a abrasar el corazón en deseos de adquirir a todo trance el oro necesario para comprar la alhaja! Y cuando cruza por el escaparate de la modista, ¡ha de dejar con la palabra en la boca a aquel magnífico vestido de encaje, cuyos pliegues parece que se mueven y la dicen que en su cuerpo adquirirían doble gracia y mayor belleza!" (194–95). For an excellent overview of the surge in publishing fashion magazines and the evolution of shops in nineteenth-century Spain, particularly in Madrid and Barcelona, see Jesus Cruz 107–30.

9. The image of the woman of fashion, the use of sartorial metaphors in *Rimas*, and Bécquer's essays on the art of dressing are discussed at length in García (2002).

10. The sartorial appearance of Álvaro de Mesía is explored in Ortiz, 61–72. For the significance of fashion in characters' portraits in *La Regenta* such as Ana Ozores, Fermín de Pas, and Obdulia Fandiño, consult Etxebarria and Núñez Puente 127–46 and Valis (*The Decadent Vision* 33–42, 50–51).

11. Also in her 1912 article "Crónicas de Madrid. (Sátira de las modistas)" published in *La Nación*, Pardo Bazán voiced her criticism of Spanish middle-class women's reckless spending on clothing and blind veneration of Parisian fashion. For more examples on the author's disapproval of the bourgeois woman's bad taste and frenzy for fashion, see Zárate 184 and Ruiz-Ocaña Dueñas 377–78.

Chapter One
Fashioning Womanhood and Making Modernity in Galdós's *La desheredada*

1. My use of the words *luxury* and *luxurious* in relation to fashion in this chapter requires clarification. Following Sombart's definition of luxury as "any expenditure in excess of the necessary" (59), I apply these terms in connection to articles of clothing and an overly fashion-conscious female to accentuate the surplus in both: the quantity and quality of sartorial goods desired.

2. For similar and the most recent interpretations of the image of a fashionable woman in *La de Bringas* and in *Lo prohibido*, see Scott 124–27 and Anderson 24–28, 51–57.

3. Garrido was, of course, not the first intellectual of his time to consider fashion as a hallmark of progress and civilization. Similar arguments were presented as early as 1839 by the director Torija y Carrese and the editor Ferrer y Valle of the journal *El Buen Tono* as summarized in Jiménez Morell 41–42.

4. See also an advertisement for parasols from 1852 in *El Correo de la Moda* in Pena González, *Traje* 251. As the description of the breath-taking selection of these items indicates, society expected women to learn to match a specific type of sun umbrella with their dresses.

5. This is not to say that Miquis's observations were incorrect, but to suggest that this scene has more to offer than has been discussed previously. For analysis of this episode see, among others, Dendle; Bly *Galdós's Novel* 4–7; and López, Ignacio-Javier 83–87.

6. It bears noting that the democratization of fashion was favored in conduct manuals also in the early decades of the nineteenth century in Spain. On the concept of a refined woman and man of non-aristocratic birth and wealth and the prerequisites for them to join the polite society, see J. Cruz 28–36.

7. As Benedetto Croce noticed, and more recent scholarship endorsed, the contradiction between tradition and novelty as well as the continuance of some traditional practices, whether in the world of politics, economy, or cultural habits, was neither unique to Spain nor made Spanish bourgeoisie less committed to the process of modernization. On Spain's uneven yet sustained progress toward modernity, see, among others, Croce 105–06, Ringrose 135–62, Fusi Aizpurúa and Palafox Gamír 11–163.

8. Already in 1874, José Selgas wondered how attractive this image of an honest and unassuming marriageable young lady was, not only to men but also to women themselves. In his essay "La última moda," Selgas wrote: "No hay nada que hermosee tanto el semblante de la mujer como la honestidad; nada que la embellezca tanto como el pudor. Convengo en ello ... pero el pudor y la honestidad son dos adornos demasiado antiguos. Mírese como se quiera, ello es que no ofrecen novedad ninguna. ¡Los lazos del cariño! ... ¡Los lazos de la familia! ... Muy bien; nada hay que decir contra ellos; pero el lazo que la moda ha hecho célebre en este momento ... ¡Oh, ese sí que es lazo! ..." (353–54).

9. For the symbolic value of Isidora's boots, see Martinelli 115–17 and more recently Blanco Carpintero (2011).

10. Also Pardo Bazán in *La Tribuna* (1882) provided a pessimistic portrait of a seamstress, Caramela, corroborating, thus, that this type of occupation bound women to hard work, poverty, and a lack of appreciation. "—¡La de las puntillas! —exclamó doña Dolores—. ¡Buena pieza! Ahora las hacéis muy mal, tú y tu tía ... Ponéis hilo muy gordo. —¡Se ve tan poco! ... ¡Los días son tan cortos! Y tiene una las manos frías; en hacer una cuarta de puntilla se va una mañana. Casi, descontando lo que nos cuesta el hilo, no sacamos para arrimar el puchero a la lumbre ..." (85). On the deplorable work and life conditions of the Madrilenian seamstresses, see Núñez Orgaz.

11. Male consumerism and male protagonists' interest in fashion in *La desheredada* deserves an extensive study apart. As the sartorial transformation of such social opportunists as Botín and *Gaitica*, as well as the observance of dressing etiquette of the upstanding citizens such as Miquis's father-in-law, Muñoz y Nones, shows, men also were involved, albeit, perhaps in a more discreet manner than women, in forging and/or preserving the desirable social identity through the art of dressing.

Chapter Two
What Is a Man of Fashion? Manuel Pez and the Dandy in Galdós's *La de Bringas*

1. Shortly thereafter, Galdós experimented again with the figure of the *señorito* by creating the personage of Juanito Santa Cruz in *Fortunata y Jacinta* (1886).

2. See Benjamin, *The Paris of the Second Empire in Baudelaire* (124–25), *The Arcades Project* (806), and Kracauer, *Orpheus in Paris: Offenbach and the Paris of His Time* (68–69). For more on Benjamin's and Kracauer's descriptions of the dandy as a modern urban phenomenon, consult Gilloch (153–54) and Wilson (*The Invisible* 4).

3. An exception is Gabriel Cabrejas, who in 1991 in his study "Galdós: Una enciclopedia de hombres inútiles," mentioned Manuel Pez as a figure that combines three characteristics of the dandy: "sentido de la elegancia ... seguridad en sí mismo y facilidad de palabra" (178). Cabrejas's essay, however, does not focus on Manuel Pez and does not analyze any of these three characteristics in Galdós's portrait of Pez in *La de Bringas*.

4. See also Pedro Galindo, in *Verdades morales en que se reprenden, y condenan los trajes vanos, superfluos y profanos; con otros vicios y abusos que hoy se usan; mayormente los escotados deshonestos de las mujeres* (1678), who reproved upper-class men for their excessive care of their bodies. Galindo created the image of a fashion-conscious, effeminate male as indolent and incapable of performing military duties. He also associated the decline of masculine virtues with Spain's decadence, writing "luego a estos peinados les dan una bandera de capitán ... y ... se pierde la plaza, la hacienda, la honra y las vidas ..." (qtd. in Vigil 197).

5. For more information on the image of a man of fashion in the writings of the sixteenth- and seventeenth-century moralists and social commentators, see Vigil (194–97). On the figure of *petimetre* and the eighteenth-century man's attraction to sartorial finery, consult Kany (174–88), Martín Gaite (72–76), and Haidt, *Embodying Enlightenment* 107–20 and *Women, Work and Clothing* 58–61.

6. See Antonio Torquemada, *Colloquios satíricos* (1522), Juan de Zabaleta's essay "El Galán" in *El día de la fiesta por la mañana y por la tarde* (1654) as well as Clavijo y Fajardo, *Vida ociosa de algunos caballeros* (1762) and Ramón de la Cruz, *El petimetre* (1764).

7. The rise of ready-made clothing for men is discussed at length in Chenoune (67–70). See also Perrot (36–57).

8. As the nineteenth century progressed, this type of advice became more common. In 1892, for instance, José de Castro y Serrano, a columnist for the popular magazine *Blanco y Negro*, explained to men the need to dye their hair in the following way: "Las canas son un signo de vejez que aflige al que lo lleva, y no satisface al que lo mira. Ser viejo es dejar de ser hombre, lo cual no todos los hombres tienen el valor de consentirlo. Teñirse, por consiguiente, las canas, es perpetuar la juventud" (8).

9. In "Los pollos de 1850," Flores described a fashionable male's wardrobe as follows: "El pollo verdadero tiene la *toilette* de *negligé* al levantarse, la de *matinée* a la hora de almorzar y la de *soirée*. … El criado sabe bien las horas de esas tres revistas de policía interior y exterior, y las prendas que convienen alistar para cada una de ellas, y prepara: para la primera, las pantuflas; el *echarpe*, la *robe de chambre* y el *bonnet*; para la segunda, las botas a la *écuyère*, el *chaquet* y la *fouet*, y para la última, el *habit noir*, el pantalón de color y corbatas a *volonté*" (141; Flores's italics).

10. Interestingly, the confusion and the derogatory meaning associated with the word *dandy* did not disappear until the last decades of the past century in Spain. On changes in definition of the term in the dictionary of the *Real Academia Española* from 1927 until 1983, see J. Cruz's note based on Russell Sebold's studies (228).

11. While a theme of frequent criticism, the dandy was also clearly a source of interest among young Spaniards throughout the nineteenth century. In 1836, in the magazine *Semanario pintoresco*, an anonymous author wrote: "La influencia inglesa va ganando terreno visiblemente en nuestra España … los elegantes remedan a los *dandys*, montan caballos ingleses … y los sastres … corren en persona a las orillas del Támesis para contar este nuevo empréstito" (qtd. in Strbáková 808). For an exhaustive list of quotes from Spanish texts from 1833 to 1900 with references to the figure of the dandy in Spanish society, see Strbáková (808–11).

12. The presence of *levisac*, a word that, according to Strbáková, first appeared in the Spanish language in 1869 and was created "con toda probabilidad por unión de *levita* y *saco*" (369), serves two purposes in Galdós's novel. First, it re-creates the aura of 1869 Spain. Second, it emphasizes Francisco's inferiority to Pez. Because in nineteenth-century Europe one could not be considered a gentleman without wearing a frock coat and because Francisco's outfit consisted only in part of a frock coat, Pez, whose attire is composed mainly of this garment, embodies, therefore, the figure of a proper gentleman, *un hombre de levita*. For more on the etymology of *levisac* and the cultural meaning of *un hombre de levita* in nineteenth-century Spain, see Strbáková (369–70 and 29–31, respectively).

13. A man's dependence on his tailor for providing him with an up-to-date outfit/look and, consequently, for marking his social identity was well known before the second half of the nineteenth century in Europe. "Tell me who your tailor is, and I will tell you who you are," wrote the French social commentator, Jean Grandville, in 1844 in *Un Autre Monde* (qtd. in Lehmann 297). On the importance of a tailor in the men's world in the early decades of the nineteenth century in Spain, see also Manuel Bretón de los Herreros's satirical account, *Los sastres* (1835).

Chapter Three
Fashion and Femininity in Pardo Bazán's *Insolación*

1. "Asís Taboada no es nadie" (1469), wrote Clarín in his essay "Emilia Pardo Bazán y sus últimas obras," issued originally in *Madrid Cómico* in 1890.

2. For the most recent studies devoted to the symbolic use of the female body in *Insolación*, see Mayoral, Scarlett, and Valis (*Confession*).

3. Only coquettish women rely on modern cosmetics to preserve their charms, claimed Ramón de Navarrete in his essay "La coqueta" (1843): "tiñen sus cabellos cuando comienzan a blanquear, estiran su cutis con cosméticos y menjurges cuando principia a arrugarse, y reemplazan sus dientes con los que construyen Rotondo y Monasterio, cuando los primitivos desaparecen. Esas no son ni solteras, ni casadas, ni viudas, ni madres; no son más que coquetas" (39). Similarly, Moreno Godino assured his readers in *La elegante* (1871) that truly elegant women do not need to use rouge, powder, or perfumes to be considered beautiful. Whether a great lady or a country girl, "[a] ambas les repugnan los postizos, los cosméticos y los perfumes penetrantes ... la limpieza es base de toda elegancia" (Moreno Godino 293).

4. Blanca Valmont reiterated this point many times during her career. In 1895, for example, she reminded her audience again that "la mujer al vestirse y adornarse ... revela su carácter, sus inclinaciones, sus gustos" (qtd. in K. E. Davis 68). For more on Valmont's views of fashion as a vehicle for women's self-expression, see K. E. Davis (65–84).

5. The critics who most recently commented on the ambiguous nature of the novel are Gómez Madrid (2007) and Zecchi (2007).

6. Considered in the first half of the nineteenth century as a hallmark of resistance to foreign fashion (e.g., a French hat), the *mantilla* was emblematic of Spanish women's commitment to maintain their national identity, as Mesonero Romanos demonstrated in his social sketch *El sombrero y la mantilla* (1835). Although *mantillas* were less common among bourgeois and upper-class women already in the 1850s, they continued to be associated with Spain's national character and traditions throughout the rest of the nineteenth century, as Eusebio Blasco observed in his 1895 essay *Mantillas y paveros*. "Pasó el tiempo santo. Vimos en él con verdadero placer las mantillas que aumentan la belleza femenina, y veremos hoy en los toros

otras mantillas ... y siquiera por más horas, reconoceremos nuestra España abrumada y alegre, rumbosa y creyente, cristiana y torera" (Blasco 133). For more on the cultural meaning of *mantillas* in nineteenth-century Spain, consult Menéndez Pidal (472–73), Dendle (51–53), and Díaz-Plaja (83–86).

7. The female gaze, as E. Ann Kaplan contended in "Is the Gaze Male?," does not carry the same power of action and possession the way the male gaze does. However, it is the act of having looked at Pacheco that makes Asís's behavior defiant of feminine decorum. According to Perinat and Marrades, "[l]a mujer respetable debe andar por la calle y los lugares públicos sin levantar la vista del suelo; sostener la mirada y corresponder a ella ... es algo que caracteriza a la prostituta" (125).

8. Female sexuality was taboo even in nineteenth-century clinical studies. The bourgeois woman was considered asexual in the sense that she satisfied "her sexual needs, not through intercourse with the male, but through childbirth" (Aldaraca, *The Medical Construction* 406).

Chapter Four
The Sartorial Charm of the Modern Man in Pardo Bazán's *Insolación*

1. Lila Rañó de Petracchi, for instance, is one of the few critics who in her interpretation of *Insolación* does not describe Pacheco in a negative light: "Pacheco es también un personaje admirable, digno de figurar junto a Asís Taboada, ambos jóvenes, libres, vehementes y con toda España en las venas" (105). Scholars who paid particular attention to Pacheco are Whitaker and Torrecilla.

2. Also Akiko Tsuchiya referred to Pacheco's portrait in Asís's and the third-person narrator's accounts as "the evocation of the feminized dandy figure" (*Marginal Subjects* 143).

3. In her essay, Pardo Bazán observed: "También cabe decir mucho y malo de las camisas de vestir, o camisolas, como les llama la gente sencilla. Son la invención más incómoda y cara que pudo ocurrírsele al geniecillo maligno que se goza en hacer desapacible la existencia del hombre" ("Más indumentaria" 1).

4. Years later, in her column, "La vida contemporánea" (1911), Pardo Bazán again drew attention to the uncomfortable, rigid style in men's dressing by asking: "¿de qué nos admiramos, cuando el hombre viene sufriendo sin protestar la imposición del espantable sombrero de copa, y no lo ha pisoteado cien veces, enviándolo de un puntapié al Rastro, a servir de depósito de clavos viejos?" (142).

5. Pardo Bazán commented in "Más indumentaria": "La moda actual del traje masculino persiste sólo porque no hay un hombre eminente que tenga el arrojo de reformarla" (1). Many years later, the novelist reiterated this point by stating "hay modas masculinas que dañan al cuerpo y riñen con las elementales de la estética. Los varones, sin embargo, las aguantan, no dan indicios de protestar contra ellas" (*Crónicas de Europa* 688).

6. Pardo Bazán concluded her reply to her reader from Coria in this way: "Ya verá el amigo de Coria como ... el mundo no adelanta / un paso mas en su triunfal carrera, / cuando algun escritor, como yo, canta / lo primero que salta en su mollera, / etcétera. Y seguirán los pantalones tan feísimos y tan universales como hoy, y el sombrero de copa tan favorecido, y yo sin mas láuro que el gusto de decir mi opinión" ("Más indumentaria" 1).

7. "In the attire of a young man, nothing at all should attract attention, nor invite comment, except that which might be usual among honorable men" (qtd. in Haidt, *Embodying Enlightenment* 138), preached the Jesuit Pedro de León already in the early seventeenth century. Likewise, a century later, a man's care for dressing stylishly was linked to his desire to be seen and as such it was viewed as a behavior characteristic of the *petimetre*—an antithesis of a "real man." For more on the *petimetre*, his modishness, and his subversive attitude toward gender conventions, consult Haidt (*Embodying Enlightenment* 109–12).

8. Identified as an indispensable component of a gentleman's formal wear even as late as in the first decade of the last century, the *frac* served Pardo Bazán frequently to hint at her protagonists' problematic stance toward society and its approved models of masculinity. In *La Quimera* (1905), for example, Silvio Lago, despite wearing el *frac* to the theater, feels detached from Madrid society: "Tiendo la vista por las butacas ... hormiguean los fraques y los uniformes; y me fijo ... en la cantidad inverosímil de condecoraciones, placas y cruces que brillan sobre el paño negro ... Miro a mi frac enteramente liso y desnudo ... y me siento muy vacío de vanidades, escastillado solamente en mi orgullo loco de querer ser algo que no se expresa con una cinta de colores ni con un trozo de metal" (380–81). For analysis of the ways in which Pardo Bazán made use of the frock coat of the main character, Pedro Hojeda, to allude to his image as "the Other" in her short story "El frac" (1909), see M. E. Davis 36–44.

9. This is not to say that only men smoked in nineteenth-century Spain. As foreign commentators, Spanish writers and intellectuals (Díaz-Plaja 151–52), including Pardo Bazán (Zárate 185–86), attest, women smoked as well. However, while, as doña Emilia stated in her essay "Crónicas ligeras: Columnas de humo," published in *La Época* in 1896, "en toda la Península ... imposible sería ver fumar ... en la calle ... a la mujer del pueblo, menos a la burguesa" (1) and while for "señoras que después de comer enciendan con monería el suave cigarrillo turco, eso es más bien juego que hábito, y más bien *chic* que afición" (1; Pardo Bazán's italics), smoking in public was, nevertheless, a "patrimonio exclusivo del varón" (1). For more on smoking as an aspect of male tradition, see Pardo Bazán's short story "Fumando" (1909). On the connection between cigar smoking and the patriarchal ideals of masculinity, consult Hoffman, *Of Broken Fans* 401–11 and M. E. Davis 162–63.

10. "The ultimate fin de siècle touch of elegance was a flower in the buttonhole—carnation, rose ... gardenia" (106), informs the contemporary fashion historian, Farid Chenoune, in his study of men's dressing styles in late-nineteenth-century France and England. Chenoune links further the flower in the buttonhole to dandyism. "I sacrifice a rose each evening to my buttonhole; roses are the Order of the Garter of that great monarch called Nature," commented the famous nineteenth-century French dandy and theorist on dandyism, Barbey d'Aurevilly (qtd. in Chenoune 106).

11. It is noteworthy that, as Vicente de la Fuente affirmed in his social sketch "El estudiante," published in the collection of essays *Los españoles pintados por sí mismos* (1843), *el hongo* was first adopted by students as part of "el furor ... contra la orden" (99). "A estos conatos es debida la invención de *los hongos*," continued de la Fuente, "con que algunos de ellos trataron ... adornar la cabeza ... sin respetar los tiempos que corrían. Pero la sociedad ... se les rió en sus barbas y designó con el apodo de *monicongos* (monos con hongos)" (99; de la Fuente's italics). Notice that also in *La Regenta*, liberal men, such as Ana's father and his friends ("Don Carlos no tenía más amistad que la de unos cuantos hongos, filosofastros y conspiradores" [1: 262]) or those who like to appear liberal, such as Marqués de Vegallana ("La sencilla americana y el hongo ... eran la garantía de su popularidad en las aldeas" [1: 382]) wore this type of hat. Unlike the transition from *la capa* to *el gabán*, the change from a top hat to a bowler was a subject of long and passionate debate among nineteenth-century writers and intellectuals. For arguments in favor and contra *el hongo*, see the collection of essays, poems, and theatrical plays written by various authors and assembled in *Sombrero. Su pasado, su presente y su porvenir* (1859). For a wealth of observations on men's transition from *la capa* to *el gabán* penned by Mesonero Romanos, José Puiggarí, and other nineteenth-century intellectuals, consult Pena González, *Traje* 212–14.

12. Spanish writers and foreign commentators frequently shared the observation that as late as in the last decades of the nineteenth century wearing a top hat was a sign of the Spanish man's adherence to tradition and a mark of distinction and importance in society. Even Pérez Galdós, who on more than one occasion expressed openly his disapproval of the top hat, admitted, albeit somewhat ironically, in *Fortunata y Jacinta* (1887) the following: "El sombrero de copa da mucha respetabilidad a la fisonomía, y raro es el hombre que no se cree importante sólo con llevar sobre la cabeza un cañón de chimenea" (1: 151). As the French commentator E. Muret noted in *Un hiver en Espagne* (1893), only men who overtly cared less about the qualities that the top hat could confer upon them or "los de menos importancia, jóvenes y extranjeros, se conforman con el 'melón'" (qtd. in Díaz-Plaja 80).

13. In his *Higiene del matrimonio o El libro de los casados,* Monlau cautioned: *"Lo que da la vida, sirve también para conservarla.* ... [No es extraño, por lo tanto, que] el abuso de la copulación dé por resultados, en el hombre, la debilidad de los genitales, la emisión involuntaria del semen, la atrofia de los testículos ... tales son los amargos frutos de los excesos en la copulación." (Monlau's italics, qtd. in Jagoe, *La mujer en los discursos* 393–94). For more on the connection between the excessive sexual activities and the peril of losing "manhood" in the manuals by various nineteenth-century social hygienists in Spain, consult Jagoe, *La mujer en los discursos* 321–22. For this link in the portrait of other male characters in the nineteenth-century Spanish narrative, i.e., Pérez Galdós's Máximo Manso in *El amigo Manso* (1882), see Copeland 114–15.

Chapter Five
Dressing the New Woman in Picón's *Dulce y sabrosa*

1. Consider, as an example, the description of Paco Vegallana's sexual excitement while looking at Obdulia's feet adorned in fancy stockings in Clarín's *La Regenta* (1884–85): "Obdulia había tropezado quinientas veces con el Marquesito ... Un movimiento brusco de la dama, que traía falda corta ... dejó ver a Paco parte, gran parte de una media escocesa de un gusto nuevo. ... ¿Por qué le excitaba más el velo que la carne? No se lo explicaba. ... Veía una media hasta ocho dedos más arriba del tobillo ... ¡y adiós idealismo! ... si la media de Obdulia no hubiera sido escocesa, tal vez el mozo no hubiese perdido la tranquilidad de su reposo idealista; pero aquellos cuadros rojos, negros y verdes, con listillas de otros colores, le volvieron a la torpe y grosera realidad, y Obdulia notó en seguida que triunfaba" (1: 407).

2. The significance of the foot fetish in the nineteenth-century Spanish narrative and culture as well as in the rest of the Western world is discussed at length by Lucía Etxebarria and Sonia Núñez Puente (99–146). For more on Freud's writings and recent theories on foot fetishism, consult Emily Apter (1–14).

3. A notable exception was *La Vie Parisienne*, a French newspaper founded in 1863 in which "suggestive dishabille was one of the principal themes" (Perrot 239). The first trade journal, *Les Dessous Élégants*, devoted exclusively to ladies' underwear, was launched in 1901 in Paris.

4. According to Lola Gavarrón, women's underclothes were considered unspeakable objects in fashion journals and social commentators' writings in Spain until the early decades of the last century. The first Spanish magazine with "los chiste verdes con alusiones a las *deshabillées* femeninas" (Gavarrón 194) was *Papitu*, launched in 1908 in Barcelona. The first trade journals dedicated to feminine and masculine underwear, *Miss* and *Chic*, were issued in 1932 in Madrid. Around the same time, elegant shops with French lingerie, such as *La Jouvence*, were established in the Salamanca district as well as on Montera and Carretas streets in Madrid.

5. For examples of how Spanish writers, social commentators, and artists portrayed the New Woman in the last decades of the nineteenth century, see Tolliver, *Cigar Smoke* 43–65 and López Fernández 294–97.

6. Also progressive feminist women writers, such Emilia Pardo Bazán in *Memorias de un solterón* (1896), portrayed the New Woman as a tomboy who wears (at least in the first part of the novel) men's boots, short hair, and does not care about her looks. For the sartorial transformations of Feíta Neira and the concept of the New Woman in Spanish narrative, see Charnon-Deutsch (*Narratives of Desire* 141–85).

7. On eroticization of actresses and dance-hall girls in drawings and caricatures in nineteenth-century Spanish periodicals and for descriptions of the theater in nineteenth-century Spain as a marketplace where women's bodies were items of exchange of pleasure for bread, see Charnon-Deutsch (*Fictions* 138–45).

8. According to Amando de Miguel, "la primera ola de incorporación de la mujer al trabajo extradoméstico" (167) took place in Spain during World War I. It is during these years, wrote de Miguel, when "las mujeres … comienzan a vivir por sí mismas y para sí mismas, con plena aceptación social … Trabajan como señoritas de mostrador … profesoras de idiomas … artistas de teatro, dibujantes … El movimiento era todavía muy tímido, mucho menor que el de los otros países que estaban en guerra" (167).

9. Picón was, in fact, censured by conservative critics for his liberal views on sexuality and marriage in *Dulce y sabrosa*. For these critics' comments, see Sobejano, "Introducción," *Dulce y sabrosa* 57–58 and Valis, *The Novels of Picón* 142.

10. The image of an upper-class woman in her sartorial splendor reposing either before or after a ball was frequently painted by nineteenth-century Spanish artists such as José Masriera, Salvador Sánchez Barbudo, and Ignacio Pinazo. For more on this image in these and other Spanish artists' works, consult Charnon-Deutsch, *Fictions* 230–35, López Fernández 23–24, and Pérez Rojas 139.

Conclusion

1. In fact, as Alba del Pozo García has shown in her recent study, already in the late 1890s texts such as *Alma contemporánea* (1899) by José María Lianas Aguilaniedo, "la moda se erigirá en el principal vehículo de construcción del género" (179), and most of all, as the representation of the feminine.

2. The link between fashion and gender in the modernist writings is discussed in Valis (*Female Figure* 291–96). For the role of the art of dressing in the representations of new ideals of femininity and less conventional gender relations in the Spanish narrative of the 1920s, consult Larson 282–96 and Bordonada 99–103.

Bibliography

Alarcón, Pedro Antonio de. *Viajes por España*. 1883. Madrid: Est. Tipográfico "Sucesores de Rivadeneyra," 1907. Print.

Alas, Leopoldo (Clarín). "Emilia Pardo Bazán y sus últimas obras." 1890. In *Obras completas*. Vol. 4. Yvan Lissorgues and Jean-François Botrel. Oviedo: Nobel, 2005. 1459–78. Print.

———. "Modas I." 1895. In *Obras completas*. Vol. 9. Ed. Yvan Lissorgues and Jean-François Botrel. Oviedo: Nobel, 2005. 251–55. Print.

———. "Modas II." 1895. In *Obras completas*. Vol. 9. Ed. Laureano Bonet, Joan Estruch, and Francisco Navarro. Oviedo: Nobel, 2005. 261–67. Print.

———. *La Regenta*. 1885. Ed. Juan Oleza. 2 vols. Madrid: Cátedra, 2005. Print.

Aldaraca, Bridget A. *El Ángel del Hogar: Galdós and the Ideology of Domesticity in Spain*. North Carolina Studies in the Romance Languages and Literatures. Chapel Hill: North Carolina UP, 1991. Print.

———. "The Medical Construction of the Feminine Subject in Nineteenth-Century Spain." In *Cultural and Historical Grounding for Hispanic and Luso-Brazilian Feminist Literary Criticism*. Ed. Hernán Vidal. Minneapolis, MN: Institute for the Study of Ideologies and Literature, 1989. 395–414. Print.

Alonso Morales, María del Carmen. "Los trapos en *La Regenta*." In *II Jornadas Internacionales sobre Moda y Sociedad: Las Referencias Estéticas de la Moda*. Ed. Isabel Montoya Ramírez. Granada: Universidad de Granada, 2001. 19–26. Print.

Amann, Elizabeth. "Nature and Nation in Emilia Pardo Bazán's *Insolación*." *Bulletin of Spanish Studies* 85.2 (2008): 175–92. Print.

Amorós, Celia. *Tiempo de feminismo: Sobre feminismo, proyecto ilustrado y postmodernidad*. Madrid: Cátedra, 1997. Print.

Anderson, Lara. *Allegories of Decadence in Fin-de-Siècle Spain: The Female Consumer in the Novels of Emilia Pardo Bazán and Benito Pérez Galdós*. Lewiston, NY: Edwin Mellen, 2006. Print.

Andreu, Alicia. *Galdós y la literatura popular*. Madrid: Sociedad General Española de Librería, 1982. Print.

Apter, Emily. *Feminizing the Fetish: Psychoanalysis and Narrative Obsession in Turn-of-the-Century France*. Ithaca and London: Cornell UP, 1991. Print.

Arthurs, Jane. "Revolting Women: The Body in the Comic Performance." In *Women's Bodies. Discipline and Transgression*. Ed. Jane Arthurs and

Jean Grimshaw. London and New York: Cassell, 1999. 137–64. Print.

Badenes, José Ignacio. *Performing Dandy: Manuel Machado and the Anxiety of Masculinity*. New Orleans: UP of the South, 2003. Print.

Baralt, Rafael María. *Diccionario de galicismos: Voces, locuciones y frases de la lengua francesa que se han introducido en el habla castellana moderna. Juicio crítico de las que deben adoptarse, y la equivalencia castiza de las que no se hallan en este caso*. 1855. Buenos Aires: Alfonso Ruiz, 1874. Print.

Barker-Benfield, Ben. "The Spermatic Economy: A Nineteenth-Century View of Sexuality." In *The American Family in Social-Historical Perspective*. Ed. Michael Gordon. New York: St. Martin's, 1973. 336–71. Print.

Baudelaire, Charles. "The Painter of Modern Life." 1863. In *The Painter of Modern Life and Other Essays*. Trans. and ed. Jonathan Mayne. London: Phaidon, 1995. 1–40. Print.

Bécquer, Gustavo Adolfo. "Bailes y bailes." 1864. In *Obras completas*. Vol. 2. Ed. Ricardo Navas Ruiz. Madrid: Turner, 1995. 631–37. Print.

———. "La mujer a la moda." 1863. In *Obras completas*. Vol. 2. Ed. Ricardo Navas Ruiz. Madrid: Turner, 1995. 600–05. Print.

Benjamin, Walter. *The Arcades Project*. Trans. Howard Eiland and Kevin McLaughlin. Cambridge: Belknap Press of Harvard UP, 1999. Print.

———. "The Paris of the Second Empire in Baudelaire." In *The Writer of Modern Life: Essays on Charles Baudelaire*. Trans. Howard Eiland and Edmund Jephcott. Ed. Michael W. Jennings. Cambridge, MA and London: Belknap Press of Harvard UP, 2006. 46–133. Print.

Bestard de la Torre, Vizcondesa [pseud. for Alfredo Pallardó]. *La elegancia en el trato social: Reglas de etiqueta y cortesanía en todos los actos de la vida*. Madrid: A. P. Guillot, 1898. Print.

Blanco, Alda. "Domesticity, Education and the Woman Writer: Spain 1850–1880." In *Cultural and Historical Grounding for Hispanic and Luso-Brazilian Feminist Literary Criticism*. Ed. Hernán Vidal. Minneapolis, MN: Institute for the Study of Ideologies and Literature, 1989. 371–94. Print.

Blanco Carpintero, Marta. "La indumentaria en las novelas contemporáneas de Galdós a la luz de las nuevas estructuras sociales y económicas." *Isidora: Revista de Estudios Galdosianos* 8 (2008): 21–31. Print.

———. "El siglo fetichista: Pie y calzado como técnica narrative de Galdós." *Actas del IX Congreso Internacional Galdosiano 2009*. Ed. Yolanda Arencibia and Rosa María Quintana. Gran Canaria: Cabildo de Gran Canaria, 2011. 327–41. Print.

Blasco, Eusebio. "Mantillas y paveros." 1895. In *Obras Completas*. Vol. 16. Ed. Antonio Zozaya. Madrid: Librería Editorial de Leopoldo Martínez, 1905. 129–34. Print.

Bly, Peter. *Galdós's Novel of the Historical Imagination*. Liverpool: F. Cairns, 1983. Print.

———. *Pérez Galdós: La de Bringas*. London: Grant and Cutler, 1981. Print.

Bordonada, Ena Ángela. "'Jaque al 'ángel del hogar': Escritora en busca de la nueva mujer del siglo XX." In *Romper el espejo: La mujer y la transgresión de códigos en la literatura española. Escritura. Lectura. Textos (1001–2000)*. Ed. María José Porro Herrera. Córdoba: Servicio de Publicaciones de la Universidad de Córdoba, 2001. 89–111. Print.

Bornay, Erika. *La cabellera femenina: Un diálogo entre poesía y pintura*. Madrid: Cátedra, 1994. Print.

Bretón de los Herreros, Manuel. "Los sastres." 1835. In *Artículos de costumbres*. Ed. Patrizia Garelli. Madrid: Rubiños, 2000. 139–45. Print.

Bretz, Mary Lee. *Encounters across Borders: The Changing Visions of Spanish Modernism, 1890–1930*. Lewisburg: Bucknell UP, 2001. Print.

Breward, Christopher. *The Hidden Consumer: Masculinities, Fashion and City Life (1860–1914)*. Manchester and New York: Manchester UP, 1999. Print.

Brooks, Peter. *Body Work: Objects of Desire in Modern Narrative*. Cambridge, MA: Harvard UP, 1993. Print.

Buckley, Cheryl, and Hillary Fawcett. *Fashioning the Feminine*. London and New York: I. B. Tauris, 2002. Print.

Butler, Judith. *Undoing Gender*. New York: Routledge, 2004. Print.

Cabrejas, Gabriel. "Galdós: Una enciclopedia de hombres inútiles." *Bulletin Hispanique* 93 (1991): 157–82. Print.

Cadalso, José de. *Cartas marruecas*. 1793. Ed. José Miguel Caso González. Madrid: Espasa-Calpe, 1993. Print.

Carter, Alison. *Underwear: The Fashion History*. New York: Drama, 1992. Print.

Castro y Serrano, José de. "La pintura del pelo." *Blanco y Negro*, 22 May 1892: 8. Print.

Celaya, Gabriel. *Gustavo Adolfo Bécquer*. Madrid: Júcar, 1972. Print.

Celma Valero, María Pilar. *La pluma ante el espejo: Visión autocrítica del "fin de siglo," 1888–1907*. Salamanca: Ediciones Universidad de Salamanca, 1989. Print.

Charnon-Deutsch, Lou. *Fictions of the Feminine in the Nineteenth-Century Spanish Press*. University Park: Penn State UP, 2000. Print.

Bibliography

Charnon-Deutsch, Lou. *Gender and Representation: Women in Spanish Realist Fiction*. Purdue University Monographs in Romance Languages 32. Amsterdam and Philadelphia: John Benjamins, 1990. Print.

———. *Narratives of Desire: Nineteenth-Century Spanish Fiction by Women*. University Park: Penn State UP, 1994. Print.

Chenoune, Farid. *A History of Men's Fashion*. Trans. Deke Dusinberre. Paris: Flammarion: 1993. Print.

Clavijo y Fajardo, José. "Sobre los petimetres." 1767. In *Costumbristas españoles*. Ed. E. Correa Calderón. Vol. 1. Madrid: Aguilar, 1964. 499–502. Print.

———. "Vida ociosa de algunos caballeros." 1762. In *Costumbristas españoles*. Ed. E. Correa Calderón. Vol. 1. Madrid: Aguilar, 1964. 487–93. Print.

Collins, Marsha S. "Sliding into the Vortex: Patterns of Ascent and Descent in *La desheredada*." *Anales Galdosianos* 25 (1990): 13–23. Print.

Copeland, Eva M. "Galdós's *El amigo Manso*: Masculinity, Respectability, and Bourgeois Culture." *Romance Quarterly* 54.2 (2007): 109–23. Print.

Cox, Caroline. *Lingerie: A Lexicon of Style*. New York: St. Martin's, 2000. Print.

Croce, Benedetto. *History of Europe in the Nineteenth Century*. Trans. Henry Furst. London: George Allen & Unwin, 1932. Print.

Cruz, Jesus. *The Rise of Middle-Class Culture in Nineteenth-Century Spain*. Baton Rouge: Louisiana State UP, 2011. Print.

Cruz, Ramón de la. "El petimetre." In *Sainetes*. 1764. Ed. Emiliano M. Aguilera. Barcelona: Iberia, 1959. 131–50. Print.

Cunnington, C. Willett. *Feminine Attitudes in the Nineteenth Century*. New York: Haskell, 1973. Print.

———. *The History of Underclothes*. London: Michael Joseph, 1951. Print.

Davis, Kathleen E. *The Latest Style: The Fashion Writing of Blanca Valmont and Economies of Domesticity*. Frankfurt am Main and Madrid: Vervuert and Iberoamericana, 2004. Print.

Davis, Martha E. "Ad/Dressing Modernism: Emilia Pardo Bazán's Later Short Stories (1901–1921)." Diss. The Catholic University of America, 2010. Print.

Dendle, Brian J. "Isidora, The Mantillas Blancas, and Attempted Assassination of Alfonso XII." *Anales Galdosianos* 17 (1982): 51–54. Print.

Díaz Marcos, Ana María. *La edad de seda: Representaciones de la moda en la literatura española (1728–1926)*. Cádiz: Universidad de Cádiz, 2006. Print.

Díaz-Plaja, Fernando. *La vida española en el siglo XIX*. Madrid: Afrodisio Aguado, 1952. Print.

Diccionario de Autoridades. 1723. Madrid: Gredos, 1963. Print.

Dijkstra, Bram. *Idols of Perversity: Fantasies of the Feminine Evil in Fin-de-Siècle Culture*. New York: Oxford UP, 1986. Print.

Edberg, George J. "Un estudio de don Manuel Pez, una creación literaria galdosiana." *Humanitas* (1961): 407–17. Print.

Entwistle, Joanne, and Elizabeth Wilson. "Introduction: Body Dressing." In *Body Dressing*. Ed. Entwistle and Wilson. Oxford and New York: Berg, 2001. 1–12. Print.

Espigado Tocino, Gloria. "Cómo hacerse un hombre: La pedagogía decimonónica al servicio de la construcción de la identidad sexual." *La identidad masculina en los siglos XVIII y XIX: De la ilustración al romanticismo (1750–1850)*. Cádiz: Universidad de Cádiz, 1995. 129–50. Print.

Etxebarria, Lucía, and Sonia Núñez Puente. *En brazos de la mujer fetiche*. Barcelona: Destino, 2002. Print.

Evans, Caroline, and Minna Thornton. *Women and Fashion: A New Look*. London: Quartet, 1989. Print.

Ezama Gil, Ángeles. "La mujer objeto estético: Figuraciones del marco en *Dulce Dueño* de Emilia Pardo Bazán." In *IV Coloquio. La literatura española del siglo XIX y las artes: Sociedad de literatura española del siglo XIX*. Barcelona, 19–22 Oct. 2005. Ed. Virginia Trueba, Enrique Rubio, Pau Miret, Luis F. Díaz Larios, Jean François Botrel, and Laureano Bonet. Barcelona: Universitat de Barcelona, 2005. 103–13. Print.

———. "El profeminismo en los cuentos de Picón." In *Actas del IX Simposio de la Sociedad Española de Literatura General y Comparada*. Vol. 1. Ed. Túa Blesa, María Teresa Cacho, Carlos García Gual, Mercedes Rolland, Leonardo Romero Tobar, and Margarita Smerdou Altolaguirre. Zaragoza: Universidad de Zaragoza, 1994. 171–78. Print.

Feijoo, Benito J. "Las Modas." 1728. In *La moda femenina en la literatura*. Ed. María José Sáez Piñuela. Madrid: Taurus, 1965. 67–71. Print.

Feldman, Jessica R. *Gender on the Divide: The Dandy in Modernist Literature*. Ithaca: Cornell UP, 1993. Print.

Felski, Rita. *The Gender of Modernity*. Cambridge, MA: Harvard UP, 1995. Print.

Fernández Cifuentes, Luis. "Signs for Sale in the City of Galdós." *MLN* 103.2 (1988): 289–311. Print.

Fernández de los Ríos, Ángel. *Guía de Madrid: Manual del madrileño y del forastero*. Madrid: Oficina de la Ilustración Española y Americana, 1876. Print.

Finkelstein, Joanne. *Fashion: An Introduction*. New York: New York UP, 1998. Print.

Flores, Antonio. "Los escaparates." In *La sociedad de 1850*. Ed. Jorge Campos. Madrid: Alianza, 1968. 192–201. Print.

———. "Los pollos de 1850." In *La sociedad de 1850*. Ed. Jorge Campos. Madrid: Alianza, 1968. 139–47. Print.

Flügel, J. C. *The Psychology of Clothes*. 1930. New York: International UP, 1971. Print.

Folley, T. "Clothes and the Man: An Aspect of Benito Pérez Galdós's Method of Literary Characterization." *Bulletin of Hispanic Studies* 49 (1972): 30–39. Print.

Freixa Serra, Mireia. "La imagen de la mujer en el modernismo catalán." In *La imagen de la mujer en el arte español: Actas de las Terceras Jornadas de Investigación Interdisciplinaria*. Madrid: Universidad Autónoma de Madrid, 1984. 119–39. Print.

Freud, Sigmund. "Fetishism." 1927. In *The Standard Edition of the Complete Psychological Works of Sigmund Freud*. Vol. 21. Trans and ed. James Strachey. London: Hogarth and The Institute of Psycho-Analysis, 1961. 149–57. Print.

Frisby, David. "Georg Simmel: First Sociologist of Modernity." *Theory, Culture and Society* 2 (1985): 49–67. Print.

Fuente, Vicente de la. "El estudiante." In *Los españoles pintados por sí mismos*. 1843. Ed. Gaspar y Roig. Madrid: Biblioteca Ilustrada de Gaspar y Roig, 1851. 99–104. Print.

Fuentes Peris, Teresa. *Visions of Filth: Deviancy and Social Control in the Novels of Galdós*. Liverpool: Liverpool UP, 2003. Print.

Fusi Aizpurúa, Juan Pablo, and Jordi Palafox Gámir. *España, 1808–1996: El desafío de la modernidad*. Madrid: Espasa, 1997. Print.

Gagnier, Regenia. *Idylls of the Marketplace: Oscar Wilde and the Victorian Public*. Stanford: Stanford UP, 1986. Print.

Garb, Tamar. *Bodies of Modernity: Figure and Flesh in Fin-de-Siècle France*. London: Thames & Hudson, 1998. Print.

Garber, Marjorie. *Vested Interests: Cross-Dressing and Cultural Anxiety*. New York: Routledge, 1992. Print.

García, Miguel Ángel. "La mujer a la moda de Bécquer." In *Moda y sociedad. La indumentaria: Estética y poder*. Ed. María Isabel Montoya Ramírez. Granada: Universidad de Granada, 2002. 259–78. Print.

Bibliography

Garelick, Rhonda K. *Rising Star: Dandyism, Gender, and Performance in the Fin de Siècle.* Princeton: Princeton UP, 1988. Print.

Garrido, Fernando. "El lujo." *El Nuevo Pensil de Iberia,* 20 Oct. 1857. Print.

Gavarrón, Lola. *Piel de ángel. Historia de la ropa femenina.* Barcelona: Tusquets, 1982. Print.

Gilbert, Sandra M., and Susan Gubar. "Cross-Dressing and Re-Dressing: Transvestism as Metaphor." *No Man's Land: The Place of the Woman Writer in the Twentieth Century.* Vol. 2. New Haven and London: Yale UP, 1989. 324–76. Print.

Gilloch, Graeme. *Myth and Metropolis: Walter Benjamin and the City.* Cambridge: Polity, 1988. Print.

Gold, Hazel. "'Ni soltera, ni viuda, ni casada': Negación y exclusión en las novelas femeninas de Jacinto Octavio Picón." *Ideologies and Literature: Journal of Hispanic and Lusophone Discourse Analysis* 4.17 (1983): 63–77. Print.

Gómez Madrid, Benito. "Las ambivalencias del triángulo nacionalista en *Insolación.*" *Alba de América* 49/50 (July 2007): 151–66. Print.

Greenblatt, Stephen. *Renaissance Self-Fashioning: From More to Shakespeare.* 1980. Chicago and London: U of Chicago P, 2005. Print.

Haidt, Rebecca. *Embodying Enlightenment: Knowing the Body in Eighteenth-Century Spanish Literature and Culture.* New York: St. Martin's, 1998. Print.

———. *Women, Work and Clothing in Eighteenth-Century Spain.* Oxford: Voltaire Foundation, 2011. Print.

Heath, Elena J. "A Dandy's Evolution from Satirist to Romantic Ironist in Three *Artículos de costumbres* of Mariano José Larra." MA Thesis. U of North Carolina at Chapel Hill, 1997. Print.

Hemingway, Maurice. *Emilia Pardo Bazán: The Making of a Novelist.* Cambridge: Cambridge UP, 1983. Print.

Hoffman, Joan M. "Of Broken Fans and Cigarette Butts: Emilia Pardo Bazán Jostles the Traditional Courtship Plot." *Hispanic Journal* 22.2 (2001): 401–11. Print.

———. "¿Qué era?: La imagen del vestido en *La desheredada.*" *Romance Notes* 15.1 (Fall 2004): 125–28. Print.

Hollander, Anne. *Seeing through Clothes.* New York: Viking, 1978. Print.

———. *Sex and Suits: The Evolution of Modern Dress.* New York: Knopf, 1994. Print.

Jaffe, Catherine. "El motivo del espejo en *La desheredada.*" *Selected Proceedings of the Mid-America Conference on Hispanic Literature.* Lincoln, NE: Society of Spanish and Spanish-American Studies, 1986. 33-39. Print.

Bibliography

Jagoe, Catherine. *Ambiguous Angels: Gender in the Novels of Galdós.* Berkeley: U of California P, 1994. Print.

Jagoe, Catherine, Alda Blanco, and Cristina Enríquez de Salamanca. *La mujer en los discursos de género. Textos y contextos en el siglo XIX* Barcelona: Icaria Antrazyt, 1998. Print.

Jiménez Morell, Inmaculada. *La prensa femenina en España (desde sus orígenes a 1868).* Madrid: de la Torre, 1992. Print.

Kany, Charles E. *Life and Manners in Madrid 1750–1800.* 1932. New York: AMSP, 1970. Print.

Kaplan, E. Ann. "Is the Gaze Male?" In *Women and Values: Readings in Recent Feminist Philosophy.* Ed. Marilyn Pearsell. Belmont, CA: Wadsworth, 1986. 230–42. Print.

Karageorgou-Bastea, Christina. "La figura del narrador en *Insolación*: Apertura e incertidumbre." *Neophilologus* 82 (1998): 235–45. Print.

Kessler, Marni Reva. *Sheer Presence: The Veil in Manet's Paris.* Minneapolis: U of Minnesota P, 2006. Print.

Kirkpatrick, Susan. "The 'Feminine Element': Fin-de-Siècle Spain, Modernity, and the Woman Writer." In *Spain's 1898 Crisis: Regenerationism, Modernism, Post-Colonialism.* Ed. Joseph Harrison and Alan Hoyle. Manchester and New York: Manchester UP, 2000. 146–55. Print.

Kracauer, Siegfried. *Orpheus in Paris: Offenbach and the Paris of His Time.* Trans. Gwenda Davis and Eric Mosbacher. New York: Knopf, 1938. Print.

Labanyi, Jo. *Gender and Modernization in the Spanish Realist Novel.* Oxford: Oxford UP, 2000. Print.

Landry, Travis. "The Moral Sense of Suitors and Selectors in Jacinto Octavio Picón." *Ometeca* 12 (2008): 137–51. Print.

Larra, Mariano José de. "Los calaveras." 1835. In *Artículos varios.* Ed. E. Correa Calderón. Madrid: Castalia, 1976. 501–16. Print.

———. "El castellano viejo." 1834. In *Artículos varios.* Ed. E. Correa Calderón. Madrid: Castalia, 1976. 307–19. Print.

———. "Jardines públicos." 1834. In *Artículos completos.* Ed. Melchior de Almagro San Martín. Madrid: Aguilar, 1961. 245–55. Print.

———. "La Nochebuena de 1836." 1836. In *Artículos varios.* Ed. E. Correa Calderón. Madrid: Castalia, 1976. 549–57. Print.

Larson, Susan. "The Commodification of the Image of Spain's 'New Woman' by Mass Culture and the Avant-Garde in José Díaz Fernández's *La Venus mecánica.*" In *¡Agítese bien! A New Look at the Hispanic*

Avant-Gardes. Ed. Maria T. Pao and Rafael Hernández-Rodríguez. Newark: Juan de la Cuesta, 2002. 275–305. Print.

Lehmann, Ulrich. *Tigersprung: Fashion in Modernity*. London and Cambridge: MIT UP, 2000. Print.

León, Fray Luis de. *La perfecta casada*. 1583. *A Bilingual Edition of Fray Luis de León's La perfecta casada*. Ed. and trans. John A. Jones and Javier San José Lera. Lewiston, NY: Edwin Mellen, 1999. Print.

Litvak, Lily. *Erotismo: Fin de siglo*. Barcelona: Bosch, 1979. Print.

Longares, Manuel. *La novela del corsé*. Madrid: Mondadori, 1979. Print.

López, Ignacio-Javier. *Realismo y ficción: La desheredada de Galdós y la novela de su tiempo*. Barcelona: PPU, 1989. Print.

López Fernández, María. "Mujeres de papel: La ilustración gráfica y la imagen de la mujer en el fin de siglo." In *Mujeres pintadas: La imagen de la mujer en España 1890–1914*. Ed. María López Fernández. Madrid: Fundación Cultural Mapfre Vida, 2003. 288–97. Print.

Mandrell, James. *Don Juan and the Point of Honor: Seduction, Patriarchal Society, and Literary Tradition*. University Park: Penn State UP, 1992. Print.

Martín Gaite, Carmen. *Usos amorosos del dieciocho en España*. Barcelona: Anagrama, 1987. Print.

Martinell, Emma. "Isidora Rufete (*La desheredada*) a través del entorno inanimado." *Letras de Deusto* 16 (1986): 107–22. Print.

Matoses, Manuel. "Las que se pintan." In *Las españolas pintadas por los españoles*. Ed. Roberto Robert. Vol. 2. Madrid: Imprenta a cargo de J.E. Morete, 1872. 221–31. Print.

Mayoral, Marina. "De *Insolación* a *Dulce dueño*: Notas sobre el erotismo en la obra de Emilia Pardo Bazán." In *Eros literario*. Ed. Covadonga López Alonso, Juana Martínez Gómez, José Paulino Ayuso, Marcos Roca, and Carlos Sainz de la Maza. Madrid: Universidad Complutense, 1989. 127–36. Print.

McKenna, Susan M. "Crafting the Female Subject." *Narrative Innovation in the Short Fiction of Emilia Pardo Bazán*. Washington, DC: Catholic U of America P, 2009. Print.

McKinney, Collin. *Mapping the Social Body: Urbanisation, the Gaze, and the Novels of Galdós*. North Carolina Studies in the Romance Languages and Literatures. Chapel Hill: U of North Carolina P, 2010. Print.

Menéndez Pidal, Gonzalo. *La España del siglo XIX vista por sus contemporáneos*. Vol. 1. Madrid: Centro de Estudios Constitucionales, 1988. Print.

Bibliography

Mesonero Romanos, Ramón de. "El Gabán." In *Tipos y caracteres: Bocetos de cuadros de costumbres o el curioso parlante (1843–1862)*. Madrid: Oficinas de la Ilustración Española y Americana, 1881. 129–35. Print.

———. *Memorias de un setentón, natural y vecino de Madrid*. Madrid: Oficinas de la Ilustración Española y Americana, 1880. Print.

———. *Panorama matritense*. Madrid: Establecimiento Tipográfico de D. Francisco de Paula Mellado, 1862. Print.

Miguel, Amando de. *El sexo de nuestros abuelos*. Madrid: Espasa-Calpe, 1998. Print.

Moers, Ellen. *The Dandy: Brummell to Beerbohm*. New York: Viking, 1960. Print.

Moi, Toril. *What Is a Woman? And Other Essays*. Oxford: Oxford UP, 1999. Print.

Monlau, Pedro Felipe. *Higiene del matrimonio, e El libro de los casados, en el cual se dan las reglas e instrucciones necesarias para conservar la salud de los esposos, asegurar la paz conyugal y educar bien a la familia*. 1853. Paris: Garnier Hermanos, 1865. Print.

Moreno Godino, F. "La elegante." In *Las españolas pintadas por los españoles*. Ed. Roberto Robert. Vol. 1. Madrid: Imprenta a cargo de J.E. Morete, 1871. 289–95. Print.

Moreno Hernández, Carlos. "Bécquer, *Rimas*: Bohemia, Dandismo, Cursilería." *El Gnomo* 2 (1993): 41–50. Print.

Moreto, Agustín. *El lindo don Diego*. 1662. Ed. Frank P. Casa and Berislav Primorac. Madrid: Cátedra, 1978. Print.

Mosse, George L. *The Image of Man: The Creation of Modern Masculinity*. New York and Oxford: Oxford UP, 1996. Print.

Mulvey, Laura. "Visual Pleasure and Narrative Cinema." In *Visual and Other Pleasures*. Bloomington and Indianapolis: Indiana UP, 1989. 14–26. Print.

Muñoz, Sara. "Dime qué llevas y te diré quién eres: Vestido e identidad social en la literatura peninsular del XIX." *Monographic Review* 25 (2009): 71–88. Print.

Navarrete, Ramón de. "La coqueta." In *Los españoles pintados por sí mismos*. 1843. Madrid: Biblioteca Ilustrada de Gaspar y Roig, 1851. 36–40. Print.

———. "El elegante." *Los españoles pintados por sí mismos*. 1843. Madrid: Biblioteca Ilustrada de Gaspar y Roig, 1851. 157–60. Print.

Núñez Florencio, Rafael. *Tal como éramos: España hace un siglo*. Madrid: Espasa-Calpe, 1998. Print.

Núñez Orgaz, Adela. "Las modistillas de Madrid, tradición y realidad (1884–1920)." In *La sociedad madrilène durante la Restauración. 1876–1931.* Ed. Ángel Bahamonde Magro and Luis Enrique Otero Carvajal. Vol. 2. Madrid: Alfoz-Comunidad Autónoma de Madrid–Universidad Complutense de Madrid, 1989. 435–50. Print.

Ofek, Galia. *Representations of Hair in Victorian Literature and Culture.* Farnham, UK: Ashgate, 2009. Print.

Ortiz, Gloria. *The Dandy and the Señorito: Eros and Social Class in the Nineteenth-Century Novel.* New York and London: Garland, 1991. Print.

Palley, Julian. *El laberinto y la esfera: Estudios sobre la novela moderna.* Madrid: Ínsula, 1978. Print.

Pardo Bazán, Emilia. "La clase media." 1890. In *Emilia Pardo Bazán: La mujer española y otros escritos.* Ed. Guadalupe Gómez-Ferrer. Madrid: Cátedra, 1999. 99–107. Print.

———. "Crónicas ligeras: Columnas de humo." *La Época*, 1 Aug. 1896. Print.

———. "Crónicas de Europa: La indumentaria femenina." 1912. in *Emilia Pardo Bazán: La obra periodística completa en La Nación de Buenos Aires (1878–1921).* TVol. 1. Ed. Juliana Sinovas Maté. Coruña: Diputación Provincial de Coruña, 1999. 687–91. Print.

———. "Crónicas de Madrid. (Sátira de las modistas.)" 1912. In *Emilia Pardo Bazán: Crónicas en "La Nación" de Buenos Aires (1909–1921).* Ed. Cyrus DeCoster. Madrid: Pliegos, 1994. 141–46. Print.

———. *Cuarenta días en la Exposición.* Madrid: V. Prieto, 1901. Print.

———. *Insolación.* 1889. Ed. Ermitas Penas Varela. Madrid: Cátedra, 2001. Print.

———. "Más indumentaria." *El Imparcial*, 1 Dec. 1890. Print.

———. "La mujer española." 1890. In *Emilia Pardo Bazán: La mujer española y otros escritos.* Ed. Guadalupe Gómez-Ferrer. Madrid: Cátedra, 1999. 83–116. Print.

———. *Al pie de la Torre Eiffel.* Madrid: La España, 1889. Print.

———. *La Quimera.* 1905. Ed. Marina Mayoral. Madrid: Cátedra, 1991. Print.

———. "Reforma racional del traje en los Estados Unidos." *El Imparcial*, 17 Nov. 1890. Print

———. *La Tribuna.* 1882. Ed. Benito Varela Jácome. Madrid: Cátedra, 2002. Print.

Bibliography

Pardo Bazán, Emilia. "La vida contemporánea." *La Ilustración Artística*, 27 Feb. 1911. Print.

———. "La vida en verano. —Cuestión de ropa: San Lorenzo mártir." *La Ilustración Artística*, 20 Aug. 1900. Print.

Parsons, Deborah L. *A Cultural History of Madrid: Modernism and the Urban Spectacle*. Oxford and New York: Berg, 2003. Print.

Pena González, Pablo. *El traje en el Romanticismo y su proyección en España, 1828–1868*. Madrid: Ministerio de Cultura, 2008. Print.

———. "Indumentaria en España: El periodo isabelino (1830–1968)." *Indumenta: Revista del Museo del Traje* 0 (2007): 95–106.

Penas Varela, Ermitas, ed. *Insolación*. By Emilia Pardo Bazán. 1889. Madrid: Cátedra, 2001. Print.

Pereda, José María de. "Las comezones de la señora Pardo Bazán." 1891. In *Emilia Pardo Bazán: Obras completas*. Vol. 3. Madrid: Aguilar, 1973. 1006–15. Print.

———. "La mujer del ciego, ¿para quién se afeita?" 1870. In *Obras completas*. Vol. 7. Madrid: Librería General de Victoriano Suárez, 1922. 169–85. Print.

Pérez Galdós, Benito. *La desheredada*. 1881. Ed. Germán Gullón. Madrid: Cátedra, 2000. Print.

———. "El elegante." 1893. *Fisonomías sociales. Obras inéditas*. Vol. 1. Madrid: Renacimiento, 1923. 231–42. Print.

———. *Fortunata y Jacinta*. 2 vols. 1887. Ed. Francisco Caudet. Madrid: Cátedra, 1992. Print.

———. *La de Bringas*. 1884. Ed. Alda Blanco and Carlos Blanco Aguinaga. Madrid: Cátedra, 1985. Print.

———. *Tormento*. 1884. Ed. Eamonn J. Rodgers. Oxford and New York: Pergamon, 1977. Print.

———. "Vida de sociedad." 1893. *Fisonomías sociales. Obras inéditas*. Vol. 1. Madrid: Renacimiento, 1923. 120–26. Print.

Pérez Rojas, Francisco Javier. *Ignacio Pinazo: Los inicios de la pintura moderna*. Madrid: Fundación Cultural Mapfre Vida, 2005. Print.

Perinat, Adolfo, and María Isabel Marrades. *Mujer, prensa, y sociedad en España 1800–1939*. Madrid: Centro de Investigaciones Sociológicas, 1980. Print.

Perrot, Philippe. *Fashioning the Bourgeoisie: A History of Clothing in the Nineteenth Century*. Trans. Richard Bienvenu. Princeton: Princeton UP, 1994. Print.

Picón, Jacinto Octavio. *Dulce y sabrosa*. 1891. Ed. Gonzalo Sobejano. Madrid: Cátedra, 1990. Print.

Pozo García, Alba del. "Cuerpos escritos, textos vestidos: Moda y género en el fin de siglo español." *Journal of Spanish Cultural Studies* 12.2 (2011): 177–95. Print.

Quijano, Gabriel. *Vicios de las tertulias y concurrencias del tiempo; excesos y perjuicios de las conversaciones del día, llamadas por otro nombre, cortejos: Descubiertos, demostrados y confutados en seis conversaciones entre un eclesiástico, y una dama, o señora distinguida*. Barcelona: Juan Sellent, 1785. Print.

Rañó Petracchi de, Lilia. *La Condesa de Pardo Bazán: Su vida y su obra*. Buenos Aires: Hachette, 1946. Print.

Rementería y Fica, Mariano de, ed. and trans. *El hombre fino al gusto del día o Manual completo de urbanidad, cortesía y buen tono*. Madrid: Imprenta de Moreno, 1830. Print.

Ringrose, David R. *Spain, Europe, and the "Spanish Miracle," 1700–1900*. Cambridge: Cambridge UP, 1996. Print.

Rodríguez-Solís, E. *Majas, manolas y chulas: Historia, tipos y costumbres de ataño y ogaño*. Madrid: Imprenta de Fernando Cao y Domingo de Vai, 1886. Print.

Romero del Alamo, Manuel. *Efectos perniciosos del lujo: Las cartas de D. Manuel Romero del Alamo al Memorial Literario de Madrid (1789)*. 1789. Ed. Elvira Martínez Chacón. Oviedo: Publicaciones Universidad de Oviedo, 1985. Print.

Ruiz-Ocaña Dueñas, Eduardo. *La obra periodística de Emilia Pardo Bazán en La Ilustración Artística de Barcelona (1895–1916)*. Madrid: Fundación Universitaria Española, 2004. Print.

Sánchez Llama, Íñigo. *Galería de escritoras isabelinas: La prensa periódica entre 1833 y 1895*. Madrid: Cátedra, 2000. Print.

Scanlon, Geraldine M. *La polémica feminista en la España contermporánea (1868–1974)*. Trans. Rafael Mazarrasa. Madrid: Akal, 1986. Print.

Scari, Robert M. "Modalidades de la ironía en *Insolación*." *Revista Hispánica Moderna* 3 (1974–75): 85–93. Print.

Scarlett, Elizabeth. *Under Construction: The Body in Spanish Novels*. Charlottesville: UP of Virginia, 1994. Print.

Scott, Paddy. *Women in the Novels of Benito Pérez Galdós and Eça de Queiroz*. Lewiston, NY: Edwin Mellen, 2007. Print.

Sebold, Russell P. "Introduction." In *Rimas*. By Gustavo Adolfo Bécquer. Madrid: Espasa-Calpe, 1989. 9–157. Print.

Bibliography

Selgas, José. "El lujo de las mujeres." 1871. In *Delicias del nuevo paraíso recogidas al vapor en el siglo de la electricidad*. Madrid: Imprenta de A. Pérez Dubrull, 1887. 103–08. Print.

———. "La última moda." 1874. In *Cosas del día*. Madrid: Imprenta de A. Pérez Dubrull, 1887. 349–59. Print.

———. "Vista exterior." *Fisonomías contemporáneas*. 1877. Madrid: Imprenta de A. Pérez Dubrull, 1889. 11–20. Print.

Sempere y Guarinos, Juan. *Historia del lujo y de las leyes suntuarias de España*. 1788. Ed. Juan Rico Jiménez. Madrid and Valencia: Institució Alfons el Magnànim and Diputació de València, 2000. Print.

Servén, Carmen. "La mujer a la moda en la obra novelística de José María de Pereda y Juan Valera: Dos opiniones divergentes." In *Actas del IX Simposio de la Sociedad Española de Literatura General y Comparada*. Ed. Túa Blesa, Teresa María Cacho, Carlos García Gual, Mercedes Rolland, Leonardo Romero Tobar, and Margarita Smerdou Altolaguirre. Zaragoza: Universidad de Zaragoza, 1994. 371–75. Print.

Shoemaker, William H. *Las cartas desconocidas de Galdós en La Prensa de Buenos Aires*. Madrid: Cultura Hispánica, 1973. Print.

Showalter, Elaine. *Sexual Anarchy: Gender and Culture at the Fin de Siècle*. New York: Viking, 1990. Print.

Sieburth, Stephanie. *Inventing High and Low: Literature, Mass Culture, and Uneven Modernity in Spain*. Durham and London: Duke UP, 1994. Print.

Silverman, Debora. "The 'New Woman,' Feminism, and the Decorative Arts in Fin-de-Siècle France." In *Eroticism and the Body Politics*. Ed. Lynn Hunt. Baltimore: Johns Hopkins UP, 1990. 144–64. Print.

Sinovas Maté, Juliana. *Emilia Pardo Bazán: La obra periodística completa en "La Nación" de Buenos Aires (1879–1921)*. Coruña: Diputación Provincial de Coruña, 1999. Print.

Sinués de Marco, María del Pilar. *Mujer en nuestros días*. Madrid: Agustín Jubra, 1878. Print.

Smith, Paul Julian. "Galdós, Valera, Lacan." *The Body Hispanic: Gender and Sexuality in Spanish and Spanish American Literature*. Oxford: Clarendon, 1989. 69–104. Print.

Sobejano, Gonzalo. "Introducción." In *Dulce y sabrosa*. By Jacinto Octavio Picón. 1891. Madrid: Cátedra, 1990. 13–58. Print.

———. "Introduction." In *Moral Divorce and Other Stories*. By Jacinto Octavio Picón. Trans. Robert M. Fedorchek. Lewisburg: Bucknell UP, 1995. 17–24. Print.

Sombart, Werner. *Luxury and Capitalism*. 1913. Ann Arbor: U of Michigan P, 1967. Print.

Steele, Valerie. *The Corset: A Cultural History*. New Haven and London: Yale UP, 2001. Print.

———. *Fetish: Fashion, Sex and Power*. New York and Oxford: Oxford UP, 1996. Print.

———. *Paris. Fashion. A Cultural History*. 1988. Oxford and New York: Berg, 1998. Print.

Strbáková, Radana. "Procesos de cambio léxico en el español del siglo XIX: El vocabulario de la indumentaria." Diss. Universidad de Granada, 2007. Print.

Tolliver, Joyce. *Cigar Smoke and Violet Water: Gendered Discourse in the Stories of Emilia Pardo Bazán*. Lewisburg: Bucknell UP, 1998. Print.

———. "Knowledge, Desire and Syntactic Empathy in Pardo Bazán's *La novia fiel*." *Hispania* 72.4 (Dec. 1989): 909–18. Print.

———. "'La que entrega la mirada, lo entrega todo': The Sexual Economy of the Gaze in Pardo Bazán's *La Mirada*." *Romance Languages Annual 1992* 4 (1993): 620–26. Print.

———. "Narrative Accountability and Ambivalence: Feminine Desire in *Insolación*." *Revista de Estudios Hispánicos* 23.2 (May 1989): 103–18. Print.

Torquemada, Antonio de. *Colloquios satíricos*. Bilbao: Mathias Mares, 1584. Print.

Torrecilla, Jesús. "Un país poético y una polémica: Las interioridades de *Insolación*." *Hispanic Review* 71.2 (2003): 253–70. Print.

Tsuchiya, Akiko. "The Construction of the Female Body in Galdós's *La de Bringas*." *Romance Quarterly* 40 (1993): 35–47. Print.

———. *Marginal Subjects: Gender and Deviance in Fin-de-Siècle Spain*. Toronto: U of Toronto P, 2011. Print.

Tubert, Silvia. "Rosalía de Bringas: El erotismo de los trapos." *Bulletin of Hispanic Studies* [Glasgow] 74 (1997): 371–87. Print.

Umbral, Francisco. *Larra: Anatomía de un dandy*. Madrid: Alfaguara, 1965. Print.

Valdés Sánchez, Ivón. "La mujer moderna en la olvidada narrativa de un autor decimonónico profeminista: Jacinto Octavio Picón." *Dicenda: Cuadernos de Filología Hispánica* 20 (2002): 343–53. Print.

Valera, Juan. *Las ilusiones del doctor Faustino*. 1875. Ed. Cyrus C. DeCoster. Madrid: Castalia, 1970. Print.

Valis, Noël. "Confession and the Body in Emilia Pardo Bazán's *Insolación*." 1997. In *Reading the Nineteenth-Century Spanish Novel: Selected Essays*. Newark: Juan de la Cuesta, 2005. 235–56. Print.

———. *The Culture of Cursilería: Bad Taste, Kitsch, and Class in Modern Spain*. Durham and London: Duke UP, 2002. Print.

———. *The Decadent Vision in Leopoldo Alas: A Study of "La Regenta" and "Su único hijo."* Baton Rouge and London: Louisiana State UP, 1981. Print.

———. "The Female Figure and Writing in *fin de siglo* Spain." 1989. In *Reading the Nineteenth-Century Spanish Novel: Selected Essays*. Newark: Juan de la Cuesta, 2005. 291–305. Print.

———. "Introduction." *Sweet and Delectable*. By Jacinto Octavio Picón. Trans. Robert M. Fedorchek. Lewisburg: Bucknell UP, 2000. 11–41. Print.

———. *The Novels of Jacinto Octavio Picón*. Lewisburg: Bucknell UP, 1986. Print.

Vallejo, Catharina. "Emilia Pardo Bazán, Gender, Modernity and Nationalism at the Paris World Exhibitions of 1889 and 1890." *Revista Canadiense de Estudios Hispánicos* 32.2 (2008): 453–73. Print.

Veblen, Thorstein. *The Theory of the Leisure Class*. 1899. New Brunswick and London: Transaction Publishers, 1992. Print.

Vigil, Mariló. "La importancia de la moda en el barroco." *Actas de las Cuartas Jornadas de Investigación Interdisciplinaria. Literatura y Vida Cotidiana*. Ed. María Ángeles Durán and José Antonio Rey. Zaragoza: Universidad Autónoma de Madrid, 1987. 187–201. Print.

Villena, Antonio Luis de. *Corsarios de guante amarillo*. Barcelona: Tusquets, 1983. Print.

Weber, Max. *The Protestant Ethic and the Spirit of Capitalism*. 1905. Trans. and introd. Stephen Kalberg. New York and Oxford: Oxford UP, 2011. Print.

Whitaker, Daniel S. "Artificial Order: Closure in Pardo Bazán's *Insolación*." *Romance Quarterly* 35 (1988): 359–65. Print.

Wilson, Elizabeth. *Adorned in Dreams: Fashion and Modernity*. Los Angeles: U of California P, 1985. Print.

———. "The Invisible Flâneur." *New Left Review* 191 (1992): 90–110. Print.

Wright, Chad C. "'La eterna mascarada hispanomatritense': Clothing and Society in *Tormento*." *Anales Galdosianos* 20 (1985): 25–37. Print.

Yáñez, María Paz. "Die soziale und literarische Bedeutung der Frau in der Prosa Jacinto Octavio Picóns." In *Frauenbilder. Männerwelten*.

Weibliche Diskurse und Diskurse der Weiblichkeit in der spanischen Literatur und Kunst 1833–1936. Ed. Hochen Heymann and Montserrat Mullor-Heymann. Berlin: Walter Frey Verlag, 1999. 249–69. Print.

Zabaleta, Juan de. *El día de fiesta por la mañana y por la tarde*. 1654. Ed. Cristóbal Cuevas García. Madrid: Castalia, 1983. Print.

———. "El Galán." In his *El día de fiesta por la mañana y por la tarde*. 1654. Ed. Cristóbal Cuevas García. Madrid: Castalia, 1983. 99–113. Print.

Zamácola, Juan Antonio. *Elementos de la ciencia contradanzaria para que los currutacos, pirracas y madamitas de nuevo cuño puedan aprender por principios a bailar las contradanzas por sí solos o con sillas de su casa*. Madrid: Fermín Villalpando, 1796. Print.

Zárate, Martha. *Emilia Pardo Bazán's Articles in "La Nación," "El Imparcial" and "La Época": A Bibliographic Guide*. Lanham: UP of America, 2002. Print.

Zecchi, Barbara. "*Insolación* de Emilia Pardo Bazán: Intertextualidades y parodias, hacia una escritura de la igualdad." *MLN* 122.2 (2007): 294–315. Print.

Index

Alarcón, Pedro Antonio de, 88
Alas, Leopoldo ("Clarín"), 11–13, 16. *See also* "Modas I"; "Modas II"; *Regenta, La*
   and the dandy, 41, 47
   on fashion, 11–13, 16
   and *Insolación*, critique of, 59, 77–78, 84, 124n1
Aldaraca, Bridget A., 2, 9, 23, 29–30, 84, 119n6, 125n8
Amann, Elizabeth, 78, 87
Amorós, Celia, 5–6, 23, 34–38
Arthurs, Jane, 69, 74

"Bailes y bailes" (Bécquer), 11
Baudelaire, Charles, 4, 10, 42, 55–56. *See also* "Painter of Modern Life, The"
   Benjamin on, 122n2
   on dandyism and modernity, 42, 55–56
   on fashion and modernity, 4, 10
Bécquer, Gustavo Adolfo, 10–11, 43, 120n9. *See also* "Bailes y bailes"; "mujer a la moda, La"
   and dandyism, 43
   and fashionable women, depictions of, 10–11, 120n9
Benjamin, Walter, 4, 42
   on Baudelaire, 122n2
   on the dandy, 42
Bly, Peter, 43, 54, 121n5
Brooks, Peter, 66
Butler, Judith, 19

Cadalso, José de, 119n6
"Calaveras, Los" (Larra), 42–43
capitalism
   evolving, 32
   Sombart and, 2
   Weber and, 6, 53–54
Cartas marruecas (Cadalso), 119n6
"castellano viejo, El" (Larra), 42

Charnon-Deutsch, Lou, 33, 78, 110–11, 128n6, 129n7 and n10
consumerism, 1–5, 113
   female, in Galdós, 13–14, 21–33
   male, in Galdós, 39, 46, 50–52, 122n11
   and modernity, 1, 9, 119n1
cosmetics, 9, 60–61, 124n3
   in Pardo Bazán, female application of, 15, 57, 60, 63, 65, 72–74, 124n3
   in Pardo Bazán, male application of, 82–83
"coqueta, La" (Navarrete), 124n3
Croce, Benedetto, 28, 121n7
Cruz, Jesus, 3, 117, 120n8, 121n6, 123n10

dandy, the
   Baudelaire on, 42, 55–56
   Bécquer and, 43
   Benjamin and Kracauer on, 42
   bourgeois men and, 45, 123n11
   Galdós and, 39, 41, 43, 45–50, 52–56
   Larra and, 42–43
   origin of, 41
   Pardo Bazán and, 86–87, 125n2
   señorito and, 45
   as social phenomenon, 42, 122n3
   in Spain, first definition of, 44–45, 123n10
Davis, Kathleen E., 4–5, 24, 27, 30–31, 124n4
desheredada, La (Pérez Galdós), 2, 5–6, 13–14, 21–39, 41, 113, 116, 120–22
Díaz Marcos, Ana María, 2, 8, 119nn5–6
Dulce y sabrosa (Picón), 2, 17–19, 93, 95–111, 116, 129n9

149

Index

"elegante, El" (Navarrete), 44
"elegante, El" (Pérez Galdós), 21, 45–46
"escaparates, Los" (Flores), 1, 120n8
Ezama Gil, Ángeles, 63, 95–96

fashion / *la moda*
   Alas on, 11–13, 16
   classic theories on, 2
   and consumerism, 1–5, 9, 13–14, 21–33, 39, 46, 50–52, 113, 119n1, 122n11
   and cosmetics, 9, 60–61, 124n3
   critique of, 2–3, 8–9, 11–12, 23
   the dandy and, 41–47, 55–56
   democratization of, 2–3, 27, 121n6
   Feijoo on, 8
   Galdós on, 13, 21, 46
   in Galdós, 2–8, 10, 13–15, 19, 21–29, 31–39, 41, 43, 46–56, 113, 115–16, 118
   gender and modernity, interrelation between, 4, 19, 113–18
   and luxury, 2, 22–23, 25, 50–51, 116, 119n1 and nn5–6
   and magazines, 9–10, 99, 120n9, 128nn3–4
   meaning of, 8
   and modern femininity, formation of, 4–9, 13–19, 113–18
   and modern masculinity, construction of, 4–9, 15, 17, 113–18
   and modern Spanish society, aspect of, 1–3, 9–10, 12–13, 24–25, 113–17
   and modern urban life, feature of, 1, 10, 12–13, 21
   and modernity, in Baudelaire, 4, 10, 55–56
   and modernity and modernization in Spain, 9, 13–19, 35–39, 53–56, 75, 92–93, 113–18
   Pardo Bazán on, 16, 59–60, 63, 78–81, 120n11, 125nn3–5, 126n6
   in Pardo Bazán, 2–8, 10, 15–17, 19, 57, 59–70, 75, 77–93, 113, 115–16, 118
   in Picón, 2, 4, 8, 10, 17–19, 93, 95–111, 113, 116, 118
   as social ambition, sign of, 2–3, 39, 114
   Spanish men and
     during nineteenth century, 21, 44–46, 79–81, 123nn8–9, 123–24n12, 125nn3–5
     prior to nineteenth century, 43–45, 119n6, 122nn4–5, 123n6, 126n7
   Spanish women and
     during nineteenth century, 61–64, 67–68, 124n3, 124–25n6
     prior to nineteenth century, 60–61
Feijoo, Benito J., 8
Feldman, Jessica R., 4, 87
Felski, Rita, 4, 19, 90, 119n1
Fernández Cifuentes, Luis, 22, 34
Fernández de los Ríos, Ángel, 1, 61
Finkelstein, Joanne, 115
Flores, Antonio, 1, 44, 120n8, 123n9
Flügel, J. C., 2
Fortunata y Jacinta (Pérez Galdós), 122n1, 127n12
Freud, Sigmund, 97, 128n2

"Gabán, El" (Mesonero Romanos), 44
Garelick, Rhonda K., 4, 5, 42, 50
gender
   and accepted norms

adherence to, 15, 50, 56,
65–75, 78–93
questioning of, 7, 16, 41,
52, 56, 70, 73, 75, 80,
85–86, 90, 111, 117
transgression of, 52–53,
65–75, 78–93
and alternative models of, 7,
9–10, 14, 17–18, 22,
75, 78, 81, 83, 85, 89,
90–93, 96, 102–05,
107–11, 113
contradictions of, 7, 13, 16, 57,
75, 78, 81, 87, 92, 115
crisis of, 12, 17, 39, 53, 90–91,
93
and fashion and modernity,
interrelation between, 4,
19, 113–18
and feminine decorum, 68–70,
73–74, 87, 125n7
incoherencies of, 7, 10, 16–17,
63, 78, 87, 115
order
critique of, 7, 10, 79–81, 85,
92, 113
reinforcement of, 15–16,
62–75, 78–93
subversion of, 15–16, 56,
62–64, 66–75, 78–93
patriarchal ideals of, 10, 16,
18, 36, 65–75, 82–86,
88–93, 96, 105, 108–11,
126nn7–9
and sexual mores, 5, 17, 105,
107–11, 113, 116
shifting notions of, 2, 4, 7, 10,
12, 16–17, 19, 59, 63,
115–16
uncertainties, 7, 9, 41, 104
Gold, Hazel, 101, 108–09

Haidt, Rebecca, 119n6, 122n5,
126n7
Hollander, Anne, 4, 51, 101,
114

hombre fino al gusto del día, El (Rementería y Fica), 44

ilusiones del doctor Faustino, Las
(Valera), 11
Insolación (Pardo Bazán), 2, 5,
15–17, 56–57, 59–75,
77–93, 113, 124–25nn1–
8, 125–28nn1–13

Jagoe, Catherine, 2, 23, 102, 110,
127–28n13
"Jardines públicos" (Larra), 3

Kany, Charles E., 9, 122n5
Karageorgou-Bastea, Christina, 64,
67, 85
Kracauer, Siegfried, 42, 122n2

Labanyi, Jo, 13, 34
La de Bringas (Pérez Galdós), 2,
5–6, 13, 15, 21, 39,
41–56, 113, 116, 119n5,
121n2, 122–24nn1–13
Larra, Mariano José de, 3, 42–43.
See also "Calaveras, Los";
"castellano Viejo, El";
"Jardines públicos"; "Nochebuena de 1836, La"
and the dandy, 42–43
León, Fray Luis de, 60
lindo don Diego, El (Moreto), 8
lingerie, 18
in fashion magazines, 99,
128nn3–4
in Picón, 92–102, 113
in Spain, 99
and turn-of-the-century England and France, 99
lujo. See luxury
"lujo de las mujeres, El" (Selgas),
25
luxury / *lujo*, 8, 21
commercial world in Madrid
and, 120n8
and cosmetics, 61

151

Index

luxury / *lujo (continued)*
  critique of, 8, 23
  as defined by Sombart, 120n1
  in *La desheredada*, 24, 28–29, 32
  and democratization of, 2
  and fashion, 2, 22–23, 25, 50–51, 116, 119nn5–6, 120n1
  Galdós on, 13, 21
  and male fondness for, 50–51, 119n6
  pro-consumerist arguments and, 27
  as sign of progress, 25
  and women's penchant for, 22–23, 119nn5–6

Mandrell, James, 95, 101, 110
McKinney, Collin, 26, 52, 79, 83, 119n3
Memorias de un setentón, natural y vecino de Madrid (Mesonero Romanos), 86
Mesonero Romanos, Ramón de, 1, 9, 44, 86, 124–25n6, 127n11
"Modas I" (Alas), 12
"Modas II" (Alas), 12
"Modas, Las" (Feijoo), 8
modernity, 1–4, 119n1. *See also* modernization
  Baudelaire on, 4, 10, 55–56
  and class confusion, 3
  as cultural construct, 19
  and the dandy, 42, 55–56
  and fashion and gender, interrelation between, 4, 9, 113–18
  and feminism, 34, 38
  and flaws and contradictions of, 6, 34–35
  and industrialization, 119n1
  as metaphor, 39
  new gender ideals as prerequisite for Spain's entry into, 2, 16–19, 36–38, 56, 93, 117–18
  and Spain's integration into, 2–4, 6–9, 13–14, 22, 36, 38–39, 41, 53–56, 75, 92–93, 112–17
  as term, defined, 119n1
  and tradition in Spain, contradictions between, 28, 121n7
  and urban culture, 1, 9, 13, 21, 42, 119n1
modernization, 3. *See also* modernity
  Galdós's views of, 14, 23, 35–38, 56
  need for new gender roles and, 6, 10, 14, 17–18, 23, 37, 56, 92, 115, 118
  process of, 3, 6, 9–10, 17, 19, 92, 114, 117–18, 121n7
  Spain's progress in, 14, 36
Moers, Ellen, 4–5, 41–42, 47–49
Moi, Toril, 5–6, 36–37, 118
Monlau, Pedro Felipe, 89, 127–28n13
Mosse, George, 92
Moreto, Agustín, 8
"mujer a la moda, La" (Bécquer), 10–11
"mujer del ciego, ¿para quién se afeita?, La" (Pereda), 11
Mulvey, Laura, 66, 68

Navarrete, Ramón de, 44, 124n3
"Nochebuena de 1836, La" (Larra), 42

Ortiz, Gloria, 41–42, 45, 78, 88, 120n10

"Painter of Modern Life, The" (Baudelaire), 4, 10, 42, 55–56
Panorama matritense (Mesonero Romanos), 1, 9

Pardo Bazán, Emilia, 2, 5, 15–17.
See also *Insolación; Quimera, La; Tribuna, La*
and the dandy, link to, 86–87, 125n2
and fashionable female character, description of, 63–66, 70
and female attire (hat, glove, fan, *mantilla*, shoes, veil), use of, 63–68, 70, 124–25n6
and female beauty products, application of, 63, 65, 72–74, 124n3
and femininity, changing ideals of, 15–17, 59, 72, 75
and hairdo, symbolic value of, 63, 71–72
and humor, as narrative device, 69, 91
and irony, role of, 67–69, 85
and male attire (frock coat, cape, watch, cigar, hat), 69, 82–83, 86–89
and male cosmetics (hair lotion), application of, 82–83
and male protagonist, sartorial description of, 81–84, 87
and masculinity, 17, 82–87, 89–93
on men's fashion, critique of, 78–81, 125nn3–5, 126n6
on women's fashion, 16, 59–60, 63, 120n11
Pereda, José María de, 11, 59. See also "mujer del ciego, ¿para quién se afeita?, La" on *mujer de moda*, 11
and *Insolación*, critique of, 59
Pérez Galdós, Benito, 13–15. See also *desheredada, La*; "elegante, El"; *Fortunata y Jacinta*; *La de Bringas*; *Tormento*; "Vida de sociedad"

and the Catholic Church, critique of, 54–55
and dandylike character, portrait of, 39, 41, 43, 46–50, 52–56
and fashion and female quest for agency in the public sphere, 13–14, 22, 25, 27, 32–39
on fashionable male in Clarín, 41
and female accessories (gloves, parasol), boots, and dress, symbolic value of, 25, 27, 31, 33, 121n9
and female characters' pursuit of fashion, traditional interpretations of, 2, 21–22
and female consumerism, 13–14, 21–33
and gallery of fictional dandies and *señoritos*, contribution to, 41
and male consumerism, 46, 50–52, 122n11
on men's style of dressing, critique of, 21, 46
and the Modern Parisian woman, 28–29
and modernity, Spain's transition to, 13–15, 22, 39, 41, 53–56
and progress of modernization in Spain, views of, 14, 23, 35–38, 56
on Spanish bourgeois sartorial splendor, 13, 21
and Spanish bourgeois masculinity, crisis of, 15, 52–53, 55–56, 115
and the spirit of modern capitalism, lack of, 53–54
and Weber, 53–54
perfecta casada, La (León, Fray Luis de), 60
Picón, Jacinto Octavio, 17–19. See also *Dulce y sabrosa*

153

Index

Picón, Jacinto Octavio *(continued)*
and bourgeois sexual norms, critique of, 18, 105, 107, 116
and erotic allure, 18, 97, 100–01
and erotic imagination, 97–101, 106
and fashion, importance of, 2, 4, 8, 10, 17–19, 93, 95–111
and fashionable woman, depictions of, 95–101, 103, 108–09
and female accessories, use of, 18, 97–101, 103, 105
and female nude, 101
feminine sexuality, 96–97, 102–04, 129n9
and femininity, alternative models of, 7, 102, 105, 108–11
Feminism and, 18, 96, 101, 104–05, 107, 109
and fetishism, 97
and gender, shifting notions of, 2, 7, 17–18, 93, 96, 101–05, 107–11
and lingerie, use of, 99–102, 113
and marriage vs. free union, 18, 107–08, 110–11, 116
and modernity, 2
New Woman or *femme nouvelle*, vision of, 18, 93, 96, 102–04, 107, 109–11, 113
and sexual desire, 96–97, 105
and standard ideals of womanhood, 18, 108–09
and woman's questions, 17, 96, 101, 105, 109–10
and women and theater, 105–07
"pollos de 1850, Los" (Flores), 44, 123n9
Protestantism vs. Catholicism, 53–54

Quimera, La (Pardo Bazán), 126n8

Regenta, La (Alas), 11, 41, 47, 88, 128n1
Rementería y Fica, Mariano de, 44
Ringrose, David R., 28, 121n7
Romero del Alamo, Manuel, 8

Sánchez Llama, Íñigo, 32
Scarlett, Elizabeth, 81, 124n2
Scott, Paddy, 35, 121n2
Selgas, José, 3, 25, 121n8
Sempere y Guarinos, Juan, 8–9
señorito, 41, 45, 78, 122n1
Showalter, Elaine, 102–03
Sieburth, Stephanie, 3, 13, 22, 33
Sinués de Marco, María del Pilar, 30, 32
Sobejano, Gonzalo, 95, 101, 107, 129n9
Sombart, Werner, 2, 120n1
Steele, Valerie, 28, 100

Tolliver, Joyce, 5, 60, 64–65, 70–71, 86, 105–06, 128n5
Tormento (Pérez Galdós), 3, 33, 51, 119n4
Tribuna, La (Pardo Bazán), 121–22n10
Tsuchiya, Akiko, 5, 12, 22, 32, 34, 41, 47, 53, 87, 93, 125n2

"última moda, La" (Selgas), 121n8

Valdés Sánchez, Ivón, 107–08, 111
Valera, Juan, 11
Valis, Noël, 24, 56, 64, 73–74, 95, 100, 111, 114, 120n10, 124n2, 129n9, 129n2
Veblen, Thorstein, 2, 119n3
Viajes por España (Alarcón), 88
"Vida de sociedad" (Pérez Galdós), 21
"Vista exterior" (Selgas), 3

Weber, Max, 5–7, 53–54
Wilson, Elizabeth, 4, 19, 48, 92–93, 114, 117, 122n2
Wright, Chad C., 33, 119n4

Zecchi, Barbara, 72, 78, 124n5

About the Book

Dorota Heneghan
Striking Their Modern Pose: Fashion, Gender, and Modernity in Galdós, Pardo Bazán, and Picón
PSRL 65

The importance of fashion in the construction and representation of gender and the formation of modern society in nineteenth-century Spanish narrative is the focus of Dorota Heneghan's *Striking Their Modern Pose*. The study moves beyond traditional interpretations that equate female passion for finery with symptoms of social ambition and the decline of the Spanish nation, and brings to light the manners in which nineteenth-century Spanish novelists drew attention to the connection between the complexities of fashionable female protagonists and the shifting limits of conventional womanhood to address the need to reformulate customary ideals of gender as a necessary condition for Spain to advance in the process of modernization. The project also sheds light on an area largely unexplored by previous studies: men's pursuit of fashion. Through the analysis of the richness of sartorial subtleties in Benito Pérez Galdós's and Emilia Pardo Bazán's portraits of their male characters, this book brings forward these writers' exposure of the much-denied bourgeois men's love for self-adornment and the incoherencies and contradictions in the allegedly monolithic, stable concept of nineteenth-century Spanish masculinity. While highlighting the ways in which the art of dressing smartly provided nineteenth-century Spanish novelists with effective means to voice their critique of conventional gender order, the book lends also insight into these authors' methods of manipulating sartorial signs to explore and to envision (as in the case of Pardo Bazán and Jacinto Octavio Picón) alternative models of masculinity and femininity. Threading through all chapters of the study is the idea propagated by all three of these writers that Spain's full integration into modernity required not only the redefinition of the feminine role, but the reconfiguration of the masculine one as well.

About the Author

Dorota Heneghan is an assistant professor of Spanish at Louisiana State University. She received her PhD in Spanish from Yale University and specializes in nineteenth- and twentieth-century Spanish peninsular literature and culture, gender studies, and comparative literature. She has published articles in *Anales Galdosianos*, *Hispanic Review*, and *Bulletin of Hispanic Studies*. Her current research focuses on gender relations and nation in the works of Sofía Casanova.

"This book introduces critics of Peninsular literature to the important work being done in other national literatures regarding the subject of fashion, providing an excellent context for the reading of Spanish texts."

—Alda Blanco
San Diego State University

www.ingramcontent.com/pod-product-compliance
Lightning Source LLC
Chambersburg PA
CBHW061450300426
44114CB00014B/1922